Personal Wealth

Passing on Our Legacy

by

Monroe and Evelyn Diefendorf

authorHOUSE™

1663 LIBERTY DRIVE, SUITE 200
BLOOMINGTON, INDIANA 47403
(800) 839-8640
WWW.AUTHORHOUSE.COM

First published by AuthorHouse 02/14/05

ISBN: 1-4208-2329-9 (sc)
ISBN: 1-4208-2584-4(dj)

Library of Congress Control Number: 2004195558

Printed in the United States of America
Bloomington, Indiana

This book is printed on acid-free paper.

Table of Contents

Prologue:

Together with my husband we have conveyed our family history, values and philosophies. Thanks to "The Foundation for Family Values," we have made an investment in the form of this book to protect and preserve perhaps our greatest asset – our "Personal Wealth".

This is the Broglio/Diefendorf familyLegacy that we want to give our children, grandchildren and the generations yet to come. It is a rich heritage that we believe is worth passing on. I hope that you have as much enjoyment reading these pages as Dief and I had in creating them.

— Evelyn Diefendorf

Forward:

After 25 years in the Financial Service business, Monroe "Roey" Diefendorf, Jr. came to the conclusion that wealth has relatively little to do with money. He began on a mission to go beyond the financial approach to managing wealth in a one-dimensional approach. He believed that one's wealth was multi-dimensional, in fact 3 Dimensional. This included not only Financial Wealth but Personal and Social Wealth too. In addition, he observed the power or influence that he had over the wellbeing of a client's family through his strategic financial planning. How much greater would this influence be if he embraced a 3 Dimensional approach to wealth management? Hence, the creation of The Foundation for Family Values,LLC.

You have in your hands a document that articulates the philosophies, values and beliefs of Monroe and Evelyn Diefendorf, Sr. Their Personal Wealth that has been captured and preserved on these pages is priceless. It is aLabor ofLove created for the generations that will follow them. It is aLifetimeLabor that took their sharedLives to create.

This FamilyLegacy was presented to Evelyn and Monroe Diefendorf on Monroe's 80th birthday. It was created by The Foundation for Family Values,LLC with the help of Dr. Mark Carver, the Executive Director, along with Martha and Roey Diefendorf.

We hope that as you read these pages you will get a glimpse of the riches that have been given to us all. This is truly a wealthy couple.

The DiefendorfLegacy was made possible through the efforts of:

3 Dimensional Wealth™ Publishing

The Foundation for the Encouragement & Preservation of Family Values,LLC

Diefendorf Capital Planning Associates

152 Forest Avenue,Locust Valley, NY 11560

516-759-3900

www.DiefendorfCapital.com

Chapter One
Monroe Diefendorf: The Early Years

Monroe Mechling Diefendorf was born on July 18, 1924 to Warren Edwin and Martha Catharine Diefendorf in Mount Vernon, New York. Named after his maternal grandmother, Jennie Monroe, and his maternal grandfather, Orange Judd Mechling, Monroe was the middle son of three boys. Throughout hisLife, he was always close to his brothers, Warren Edwin Jr. who was two and a half years older and Russell Judd who was seven years younger.

Reflecting on his early childhood, Monroe remembers belonging to a close knit family. The Diefendorf familyLived in Mount Vernon, a beautiful city withLovely homes just north of the Bronx. At first, theyLived on the first floor of a two-family house shared with the Zucker family—his father's sister, her husband and two sons. Of this time in hisLife Monroe states, "I had many close friends but if I had to choose a best friend, I'd say it was my cousin, Bob Zucker. Our families were close; Bob was moreLike a brother." In 1931 the Diefendorf's moved to 251 Summit AvenueLocated across the street from Monroe's grandparent's house, a grand house with columns, a five-car garage and stalls for horses.

Christian traditions prevailed in the Diefendorf household and church was an integral part of theirLives. Bishop Herbert Welch (of the grape juice family), a friend of Monroe's grandfather, had baptized his father and his two aunts. He subsequently baptized Monroe and his two brothers. YearsLater, Bishop Welch would also baptize Monroe's own children, Martha and Monroe Jr., and numerous nieces and nephews. The Diefendorf family attended the Chester Hill Methodist Church where his father was a member of the Board, and some timeLater, his mother served as the first female trustee. As Methodists, there were certain things they did not do on Sunday: no card playing, no movies, and no dancing. Monroe recalls, "I never heard one curse word in all myLife in our house, not from my brothers, nor my mother or father."

During his grade school days, Monroe served as a class officer and class secretary.Later on, he was secretary of the YMCA High School Group. However, Monroe'sLife mostly revolved around theLife of the church: Sunday School at 9:30 A.M. at the Methodist Church, worship at 11:00 A.M. at the Episcopal Church where he sang in the choir and was a soloist, Vespers at 4:00 P.M., and then back to the Methodist Church for the young people's group at 6:00 P.M. of which he was the President. Monroe and his cousin, Bob Zucker, "were the biggest movers and shakers in the church's youth group. WeLined up speakers, shows, outings and fundraisers and also had a basketball team."

Family vacations were also a part of the Diefendorf's regular routine. They generally took vacations in upstate New York where his paternal grandfather owned aLarge house in North Granville that could accommodate the entire family. The house had once been a school that he had planned to make into a hotel as it contained about one hundred rooms. Instead, it made a wonderful family retreat center that would often include employees and colleagues of his grandfather.

Grandpa Diefendorf, whose wife,Louisa, died before Monroe's birth, was very successful in theLife insurance business even though he was only educated through high school. He was very well respected and ran a close-knit office for 42 years which covered Brooklyn andLong Island. When he died in 1931, Monroe, at age seven, remembers "feeling very proud of being the grandson of this well-loved man." (See his eulogy in chapter six). As this was during the heart of the depression, his home was tooLarge to sell so it was torn down as was most of his North Granville retreat,Leaving only one wing with ten bedrooms. His real estate empire collapsed and not much was received from the sale of his properties. This was a rags to riches to rags story.

The family also made trips to Greensburg, Pennsylvania to the farm of his maternal grandfather, Orange Judd Mechling. Grandpa Mechling was a very successful farmer andLived in a magnificent home just outside of town where Monroe and his brothers would visit during the summer. Unfortunately, after his grandmother died, his grandfather couldn't get help to run the farm during WWII, help that was much needed due to his physical disabilities. HeLost the farm, came toLive with Monroe's mother and died a poor man.

Monroe's father managed a Mutual of New YorkLife insurance agency. He started as an assistant sales manager under his father. Soon after his father's death, he took over management.

In spite of being in the depths of the depression with 25% unemployment and banks collapsing, his father was doing very well. "We had a 12-cylinder touring Packard car. Carter and AnnieLived and worked for us.

4

Carter was our butler and chauffeur. Annie, our cook and house keeper."

In 1934, when Monroe was ten years old, his father fell, causing a blood clot to reach hisLung while on a family vacation to the World's Fair in Chicago. After he became sick, he was confined to his bed on and off for nine months. Monroe remembers his father running office meetings from his bedside and using a microphone to speak to the people in the New York office. In 1935, after a short hospitalization, he died at age 41. TheLoss of his father had a profound effect on young Monroe. He states, "It was very difficult for me at age ten to handle the death of my father who was a very warm andLoving father. It was a very, very traumatic experience for me and for my brothers. But time is a great healer, and after a few years I could eventually face up to theLoss."

Of his father, Monroe recalls, "he was a people person. I remember waiting at the front door at night for him to come home from work. He always had aLittle gift for each of his three sons.

Later in myLife, I became aware of my father's considerable talents. He was most unusual. Since I was an energetic and enthusiastic boy, hopefully, I gave him aLot of joy. I'm only sorry he wasn't alive to follow my business career in a business in which he and his father, my grandfather, excelled."

Following his father's death, Monroe's mother included the boys in making family decisions. The first decision the boys made was the purchase of a tombstone for their father. Monroe remembers, "We all decided on the stone and what the inscription should be. Our mother also explained to us that the more expensive stone would mean a sacrifice for us and we would have to give up some things we mightLike. She always made us a team and handled us thoughtfully, with maturity and a great deal of affection."

After Monroe's father died, the family's standard ofLiving changed dramatically. Interest rates were at an all-timeLow of 1% and the stock market had tanked. They became a very frugal family. His mother denied herself and did all the housework so her sons could go to camp, prep school and college. At this time, Monroe reallyLearned the value of money. He was also aware that his father'sLife insurance allowed his mother to have sufficient income to stay home and raise her three boys as a full-time mother.

Catharine never remarried and raised the boys by herself as a single mother. However, she was alwaysLooking for good male role models for her three young sons. Monroe especially remembers his uncle, Kenward Zucker, and two cousins, Richard and John Diefendorf, as filling the gap. John, a West Point graduate, and Richard, an Amherst graduate in medical school at the time, spent aLot of time with Monroe and his brothers and had become "our surrogate fathers."

Monroe enjoyed spending summers at Camp Agawam as a camper. He was voted the best camper in hisLast year and received "The Governor's Trophy." He then spent two years there as a junior counselor. During this time, he attended The Story Brook School on a generous scholarship, graduating with cumLaude honors in a class of 35 students. Monroe thinks it was probably at Stony Brook that he was first called Dief. "Everybody knew me as Monroe in the family. Most of my friends called me Dief and still do."

My older brother Warren hasLed a most conservativeLife, probably greatly influenced by the Great Depression. He only dated one girl in hisLife, Dorothy Kelley, the girl he married. He worked for one company. He and his familyLived with my mother andLooked out for her for 30 years until our mother passed away.

Judd hardly knew our father since he was three years old at the time of our father's death. Judd was myLittle buddy as he grew up. I am very proud of Judd's brilliant career as a scientist with an international reputation as one of the foremost experts in the field of composites.

World War II started when Dief was still a student at Stony Brook. Immediately following his graduation,

Dief entered Amherst College. He recalls, "Those were difficult years for young men in college. Every week, there were studentsLeaving for the war. It was a very disturbing influence. We weren't studying as much as we should. There were too many farewell parties. You knew you would be entering service but you weren't quite sure when."

Dief then enlisted in the Navy. A number of his friends had signed up for the "V-12" program, an officer's training school. Dief followed theirLead four monthsLater and was sent to Williams College in November 1943. He remembers, "I picked up with my friends and it was almostLike going to college because we were taking some of the same college courses that we normally would have. Of course, we did take some Navy related courses such as navigation."

After one year at Williams, Dief went to midshipman school at Notre Dame for three months where he received specialized training in radar, damage control, navigation and shipboard guns. After graduating from midshipman school, he received additional training at Hollywood Beach, Florida. Monroe remembers, "Finally the day came [in June 1945], and I was assigned to the USS Nassau, an escort aircraft carrier." During his three years of service as aLieutenant JG in the U.S.

Navy, Dief's ship traveled to China, Samar Island in the Philippines, Guam, Saipan and Okinawa.

After WWII there were few jobs available for the millions of servicemen being discharged. Of this time in hisLife Dief explains, "Struggle! I struggled. It was tough. How we ever made it, I'll never know. We used to stand inLine around a building waiting to be interviewed by some employment agency."

Dief considered entering theLife insurance business but his cousin, Stan Diefendorf, suggested he first secure another job to establish good work habits. Dief went to work for Mr. Krueger who owned Krueger's Toy Factory which wasLocated in the Hell's Kitchen section of New York City for $30 a week. His job was to pick orders for shipment to prestigious department stores. He remembers thinking, "Not much of a job for an Amherst graduate and a former naval officer."

After about a year, Dief decided to make a career change. He followed in the footsteps of his grandfather and father and became the third generation of Diefendorfs in the insurance industry. When he started in the business, "it was straight commission, that was it. I mean no salary, no draw, straight commission." Dief remembers his early years at Mutual of New York (MONY), "I workedLiked the devil for my sales unit. I was determined that I was going to be successful."

Chapter Two
Evelyn Broglio: Growing Up

Evelyn Broglio was born on December 25, 1928, in New York City to Frank andLillian Glauda Broglio. Her brother, EligioLanfranco (calledLee), was born four years earlier. The Broglio familyLived in a three-story brownstone house in New York City within walking distance of her maternal grandparents, Carlo and Clementina Glauda. The top floor was rented out to the Pitti family from Borgofranco, Italy, the same hometown as Evelyn's father. Her father had immigrated at age eighteen, and then when she was a baby, her paternal grandfather, Benigno Broglio, a civil engineer, also moved from Borgofranco toLive with them after his wife Marta had died.

In 1932, when Evelyn was four years old, the Broglio family moved to Manhasset,Long Island because they thought it would be better to raise a family in the country. Manhasset was a small town then,Later developing into aLarge and fashionable town with a strip of Fifth Avenue shops called "The "Miracle Mile." At first the BrogliosLived above The Plandome Gardens, the restaurant that her father and a partner opened in an old colonial house. Her parentsLater built the first house in Flower Hill.

Then, when Evelyn was twelve years old, her parents built a new home in Brookville,Long Island on 40 acres of farmLand on which they had already built stables and a caretaker's cottage. There they had horses and 200 miles of bridle paths surrounding the farm. There were chickens, pigs and a cow, the caretaker's pride and joy that gave 26 quarts of milk per day. As her father was an animalLover they regularly had pet dogs—English Setters, Irish Setters, Great Danes, Cocker Spaniels.

Overall, Evelyn has many fond memories of her childhood. She recalls, "My mother used to take us to the movies almost every Friday night (the movies were 15 cents). As a family we always went to the circus at Madison Square Garden every year and also to the 6-day bicycle races, as my father knew many of the contestants. The only vacation we had, with the four of us, was most memorable for me. We went to Atlantic City and Washington, D.C. and ILoved every minute of it."

Evelyn remembers her father as being a very handsome gentleman. She states: "He was a man's man andLoved outdoor activity. He was also very sentimental. He always would tell me that I was the smartest, the most talented, and the prettiest girl. Even if it wasn't true, it didn't hurt my self-image or my self-esteem or my confidence."

Her father began working as a busboy and eventually owned his own restaurant in New York City called HappyLandings. Upon moving toLong Island he opened The Plandome Gardens during the Great Depression. Twice a week he used to drive into NYC very early in the morning to do the marketing for the restaurant. EvelynLoved it when heLet her go with him. In 1946, her father opened The Swan Club on Roslyn Harbor, a restaurant which he ran until he retired in 1966. After the war the Plandome Gardens was torn down and eleven stores were built on the property since two restaurants were difficult to run. Always a savvy businessman, her father was very successful and was written up in both Who's Who inLong Island and Who's Who in New York State. Throughout the years, Evelyn's mother did all of the bookkeeping for the restaurants.

In addition, Evelyn's mother was an excellent cookLike her own mother and her father who had been the chef in the Grand Central Hotel. Evelyn especiallyLiked it when her grandmotherLet her help in the kitchen. Evelyn's favorite dish was polenta with sweet sausages cooked in wine. She states, "I guess it was one of my favorites because it smelled so good while it was cooking." When her grandmother was not cooking or doing housework, she was constantly crocheting and made many beautiful doilies, bedspreads and flower baskets. Evelyn's motherLearned many of these skills, was a fine seamstress and had been a millenary designer before having children. Evelyn states, "I was always very well dressed. As a teenager, all I had to do was draw a picture of a gown or suit or hat that ILiked and my mother could make it to a tee."

Evelyn's parents were always there for her and encouraged her in everything she did. She admits that she probably did some things her parents would not have approved of, but she was never rebellious. She explains, "I had too much respect for my parents' opinions." According to Evelyn, "it seems as if my mother was always doing things especially for my brother and me." A special memory of Evelyn is of her mother "sitting on the beach, watching us swim in the ocean or sound, when she wasn't even able to swim. At the time it didn't seem special, butLooking back on all those times, I really think it was very courageous. She wanted us to be able toLearn and do anything we wanted to, even if she was afraid."

Evelyn has alwaysLoved her older brotherLee dearly. She says, "Lee was four years older than I, and was great aboutLetting me tag along after him when I wasLittle.Lee has been good to me my wholeLife. I'm sure he has been angry with me at times, but I know heLoves me. He was a very talented tap dancer and I enjoy the memories of when we were in shows together. Most of my girlfriends fell inLove with him, as he was aLady-killer. ILost many good friends when they thought he broke their hearts."

The extended Glauda and Broglio families would often gather together for Sunday dinners and annually at Thanksgiving. Evelyn recalls, "My mother was one of eight brothers and sisters so the gatherings were quiteLarge. Mostly everyone enjoyed eating fabulous meals and then playing cards or games." She also particularly enjoyed Christmas because it was her birthday. It was a big occasion each year, and she thought that "some people felt sorry for me because my birthday was on Christmas. What they didn't know was that ILoved sharing my birthday with Jesus."

Coming from a family with many relatives and friends, Evelyn recalls going to many funerals as a child. Funerals did not effect her too badly, "as they were a celebration of that person'sLife and a time for people to related anecdotes about the deceased. Actually, some funerals were the only times when I saw some of my relatives and that was nice." Every time someone sheLoved died, Evelyn would think of the verse of one of her favorite poems. When she went to theLake country in England as an adult, she was pleased to visit Dove Cottage whereLucy GrayLived.

She Dwelt Among the Untrodden Ways
by William Wordsworth

She dwelt among the untrodden ways
Beside the springs of Dove,
A Maid whom there were none to praise
And very few toLove:

A violet by a mossy stone
Half hidden from the eye!
Fair as a star, when only one
Is shining in the sky.

SheLived unknown, and few could know
WhenLucy ceased to be;
But she is in her grave, and oh,
The difference to me!

She states, "I'm sure at a young age our finances weren't the greatest because it was during the depression and my parents had to work very hard. I don't think it affected me negatively, since I personally never felt theLack of anything necessary for my well-being. I suppose it did help me to be able to make do and be frugal and to be thankful for all the good things that have happened to me in myLife."

Evelyn was always a good student and enjoyed school. She never had a teacher she didn'tLike. She started school at age four in New York City and continued her schooling in Manhasset. She attended her first two years of high school at OurLady of Mercy Academy, a Catholic girls' school, where she was always on the honor roll, was in PopeLeo Honor Society and Arista, and received the General Excellence award. She spent herLast two years of high school at Friend's Academy, a Quaker school inLocust Valley. While there she was active in the stamp club, held offices in the student government, had several positions on the yearbook staff and played four varsity sports—field hockey, basketball,Lacrosse and soccer. Again, she excelled academically and was always on the honor roll. At graduation, she was admitted into cumLaude society and was awarded with the gold medal award for scholarship and athletics. "I know my parents were always proud of me."

Evelyn went on to Skidmore College in Saratoga Springs, New York, aLiberal arts college that she had visited with her parents. Skidmore was a girls' school then, and Evelyn explains, "it was a nice experience to beLiving among girls and not to be distracted by boys." She majored in French, minored in math, and was always on the Dean'sList.Later, she went to Mrs. Skinner's Secretarial School during the summer toLearn typing, shorthand, bookkeeping and accounting.

Chapter Three
A Lifetime Together

While at Stony Brook, Dief metLee Broglio and they became best friends. Dief metLee's younger sister, Evelyn, when visitingLee at his home in Manhasset. He explains, "I was 17 years old, she was five years younger. I remember her as being tall, notLooking 12, being very pretty and vivacious. I remember dancing with her in their basement. She was already a good dancer and I was pretty bad."

Following WWII, the pair were reunited at Evelyn's brotherLee's wedding. About two yearsLater, Dief would "pop the question." He recalls, "I wanted to make it memorable. I was visiting Evelyn at Skidmore College during the winter. There had been a heavy snow and there wasLittle traffic on the main street in Saratoga Springs. I knelt on the snow in the middle of the road and asked her to marry me."

Monroe and Evelyn Diefendorf

Dief and Evelyn were married on April 16, 1949 at The Brookville Reformed Church by Reverend J. Stanley Addis, a humble and sincere man who was a true servant of God. Dief remembers, "A few days before the wedding, Evelyn was diagnosed with strep throat and had to be heavily dosed with penicillin so that she could make the wedding." She recalls, "I felt aLittle weak on our wedding day, but happily everything turned out okay. It was aLarge wedding with six attendants and six ushers and the reception was at my father's restaurant, The Swan Club." The newlyweds spent their honeymoon at The Tides Inn in Irvington, Virginia.

At the beginning of their marriedLife, Evelyn and DiefLived with Evelyn's parents in Brookville, New York. Dief was beginning his sales career with Mutual of New York and Evelyn worked for an insurance office in Manhasset. "In fact," she states, "I made $45 a week which was more money than Dief earned at the time." Dief adds, "I only had aLittle over $1,000 when we got married. Evelyn's parentsLet usLive with them so we could save some money. We probably didn't have enough money to furnish an apartment and pay rent. Also, we didn't have a car; we couldn't afford one, so we had to use Evelyn's mother's car."

Evelyn remembers the young couple talking about having children almost immediately after they got married. "Of course we wanted children, and I always feel sorry for people who grow old with no family to be proud of." Dief remembers, "Both our families were family oriented and I suppose it was quite natural for us to want children. A marriage doesn't seem complete without children. We were blessed by two wonderful children."

Several months after Evelyn became pregnant she quit her job. The Diefendorf's first child, Martha Jane, was born June 5, 1950 and their second, Monroe Mechling Jr. (called "Roey"), was born February 7, 1952.

What is your most treasured possession?

[Evelyn] I really don't treasure possessions. Maybe we have too many. I did save my wedding dress, which is beautiful, in the hope that someday my daughter or one of my granddaughters would wear it at her wedding.

What are the best presents you've received?

[Evelyn] Becoming pregnant with our daughter, Martha. I was not supposed to be able to have children without an operation. When I became pregnant, the operation became unnecessary. I did have to rest aLot during that pregnancy, and I don't know what I would have done without my mother to make it through without miscarrying.

[Dief] My wedding ring. Because it's from my wife as a sign of our union. It's from a girl who I think is the bestLady in the world, and from someone I Love dearly.

The young family moved to their own home next door to Evelyn's parents in Brookville at the end of 1951. Evelyn's father had given the young couple two acres ofLand and had helped them build their first house. Evelyn helped draw the plans for the new house. She states, "It was a big step for us because it meant we had to have a mortgage and we wereLiving in an area where most of the people were very affluent. We made aLot of sacrifices in order toLive there, and slowly, as our finances improved, it became much easier for us. Over the years we finished the upstairs of the house, added on aLarge great room and terrace, built a pool and a tennis court. It was a great place to raise children, but sometimes I think they may have missed out by not growing up in a town. WeLived there for 38 years. We really had a wonderfulLife in our home."

ChurchLife continued to play an important part in theLife of the Diefendorf family and both Martha and Monroe Jr. completed 13 years of perfect attendance at Sunday School. Evelyn and Dief had a close-knit group of friends whoLived in Brookville and almost all attended The Brookville Reformed Church. They had children more orLess the same ages who all got together to play and swim. The Diefendorf home was a focal point for most of the neighborhood children. The adults hadLots of home parties—charades, pool parties, costume parties, and interesting programs at the church's couples club. Evelyn feltLucky because her mother was always willing to baby-sit. If she hadn't, they wouldn't have been able to afford to go out as much as they did.

During this period of time, Evelyn served as the President of the Parent Teacher Association, taught classes for the Cornell Extension Service, taught Sunday School, was a Brownie and Girl ScoutLeader, and was County Chairman of the Girl Scouts. Nevertheless, Evelyn's primary job during this period was as a homemaker and mother. Her key to successful child raising is, "Give children aLot ofLove and aLot of attention. Keep them busy. Make sure they do their work." Further, she remembers, "My kids were very good kids. It was not difficult. Martha was more of a perfectionist. Everything had to be just so. She was a very good student. Actually, Roey was not a bad student. He will tell you otherwise but he always did very well in school."

Dief: On Raising Children

- Through positive reinforcement, encourage your children
- Give them a positive outlook onLife
- Be involved with your children – in their activities, in their schoolwork
- Share with them new experiences through travel
- Give them a Christian upbringing
- Teach them to be generous and charitable with their time as well as their money; proud of their heritage; and honest in all their dealings

While the children were growing up, Dief's career was progressing. He worked in MONY's Market Development Division under Homer Wood for 18 months. He was then given a "scratch" agency to manage which meant there were no sales people. "I thought it was inhuman what the Home Office had done to me, but they had aLease on unused office space at theLincoln Building opposite the Grand Central Station, so there I was." After a while, business was coming along pretty well.

The Home Office wasLooking for a replacement for Dick Myer, a retiring manager of a successful agency. After meeting Dief, Myer called the Home Office and said, "I have the man, here's the man you want and I'll tell you why." Soon thereafter Dief received an offer to manage aLarge part of that agency.

According to Dief, "It was fun to come to work. We were more imaginative than other agencies." He was recognized for his success with many awards, including one from theLife Managers Association of New York for his dedication and devotion to theLife insurance industry. In 1984, he was selected by his peers for excellence and outstanding service to be inducted into the Agency Management Hall of Fame of the General Agents and Managers Conference. Dief was known throughout the country for his speeches on sales management subjects, was a frequent contributor to trade journals, and was instrumental in the development of training programs.

Dief built the agency into one of the best in the country. Under his direction, the agency consistently ranked in the top 10 of MONY's 175 agencies nationwide. His agency had more successful agents than any other MONY agency.

Business occupied most of his time but Dief always found time to take family vacations, play with the children, take up golf and be active in church. Probably some of his best times were on family trips. Evelyn and Dief enjoyed having Martha and Roey with them and took them on all their vacations. In the earlier years when they hadLittle money, they went to Aunt Mabel's home in North Granville or placesLike Philadelphia, Atlantic City, Gettysburg or Washington DC.Later on they traveled more extensively to many European countries as well as Japan and Hong Kong. They had great fun traveling together and many good memories were banked.

Beginning in 1979, Dief began to experience some health problems. At the age of 54, Dief underwent a serious operation followed by an infection a yearLater that "almost did me in." After a third operation the following year, he decided that he should take early retirement because "I realized I was not immortal and it was time to stop working and enjoy my family more." Five yearsLater, he retired at age 61.

The Diefendorf's purchased a condominium in Pinehurst, North Carolina in 1977 where Evelyn's brother trained his horses every winter for six months. The Diefendorf's enjoyed the condo for about twelve years before they sold it and bought a house in Pinehurst. Evelyn explains, "It just happened that in 1988, we were in Pinehurst, a rainy weekend, and weLooked at properties. Dief wanted to buy a place here, but I did not want two houses anywhere. That night, we sat down with a yellowLegal pad and put aLine down the middle of the page with plus and minus related to the decision. We found that there were aLot of pluses and only about four minuses." The next day Evelyn and Dief made an offer on a house and it was accepted. Within a year they sold the Brookville house and moved to Pinehurst. She reminisces, "I hated to move away fromL.I. because I reallyLoved it there. However, I must confess, it was a very smart move and we are very happy in Pinehurst. It is really nice to have neighbors close by and to be able to walk around in a small village."

Evelyn and Dief have always been actively involved in their grandchildren'sLives and continue to keep in touch with them as frequently as possible.

Roey and his wife Christine have four daughters:
• Ashley Elizabeth (July 15, 1977)
• Jennie Monroe (April 7, 1980)
• Whitney Elizabeth (June 1, 1983)
• Emily Taylor (June 3, 1986)

Martha Diefendorf and her husband Robert Hogan have two children (biological father: Alan McGinigle):

- KatharineLillian McGinigle (March 13, 1981)
- Steven Monroe McGinigle (March 25, 1984)

What I Love best about Evelyn

She is truly a good person! ILove to be with her. She has been, for our 55 years of marriage, an ideal wife, and a super mother for our two children and a super grandmother for our six grandchildren.

What I Love most about Dief

He is just as affectionate and considerate as he ever was—maybe even more so. He is very easy to get along with and we agree on almost every important decision that has to be made. Of course he is very handsome and I'm proud to be seen with him. I think after being married for 55 years there is no question that we made the right choice. We stillLove each other very much and feel secure in that knowledge. I think he has a good sense of humor, which is vital if you want toLead a happy and saneLife.

Chapter Four
Lifelong Interests

Dief's Interests: Singing

Singing has been an important part of Dief'sLife. His parents encouraged his singing by providingLessons from the choir master at the Methodist Church, Mr. Fowlston. In fact, at school Monroe's favorite teacher was Miss Tryon, his music teacher. "She recognized I had a pretty good voice and I sang some solos and duets at assembly when the whole grammar school would meet."

As a child, his singing voice was Monroe's "big money maker." Monroe states, "I found out the Episcopal Church paid more money than the Methodist Church. I was getting $5 a month as a choir boy which was pretty good money in those days. My spending money came from my pay as a prefect and soloist in the choir and from odd jobs in the neighborhood."

Monroe also enjoyed playing the violin in the violin orchestra for two years in grammar school. He remembers, "I took privateLessons which I disliked because the teacher pressed myLeft fingers so hard on the violin that it was really painful. However, when ILost my violin while stopping to play a game on my way home, my mother wouldn't buy me another one, thus ending a promising career."

While his children were growing up, he would teach them songs which the family would have fun singing together in four-part harmony, especially on car trips. Dief greatly enjoyed singing in the New York City Barbershop Society, where his quartet, The Manhatters, was the 1954 NYC Barbershop champions. He also sang in the University Glee Club of New York City for 35 years and went with the Glee Club on five European tours. He continues to sing with the Golf Capital Chorus at Pinehurst and also in a quartet called the Sandbaggers.

Dief's Interests: Sports

As a child, Monroe's favorite sport was baseball and his favorite team was the New York Yankees; he knew every player, their batting averages and pitching records. Monroe played in the midget and juniorLeagues in Mount Vernon and especially remembers pitching against Ralph Branca who went on to become a star pitcher for the Brooklyn Dodgers and the New York Yankees. He also has fond memories of his father taking the family to football games at West Point where his cousin John Diefendorf attended "the Point."

When at the family retreat in North Granville, heLoved to fish, swim, canoe and camp on the Metowee River. He alsoLoved to climb a nearby mountain called "The Pinnacle" and swim atLake St. Catherine.

Monroe remembers being highly competitive in all sports, whether it was playing marbles, Yo-Yo, flipping baseball cards, or team sports. He was excellent at ping pong, horse shoes, baseball, badminton and riflery. He was good at tennis, basketball, football, swimming and volleyball. At his own admission, he wasLousy at boxing, wrestling and ice-skating.

He worked hard withLots of practice in order to excel at any sport he played. HeLearned to play many sports at Camp Agawam including riflery where he received many National Rifle Association Medals. At Stony Brook he played on the varsity football, basketball, baseball and tennis teams.

While in the Navy, he played badminton with the ship's captain on the hangar deck; the rolling and pitching of the ship made the game quite interesting. Dief took up golf at age 38, still plays regularly at age 80, and shot his age when he was 78. Even today, he continues to be competitive in sports. Playing sports and staying fit have always been important to Dief. He thinks that it is a good idea to establish a routine that becomes automatic because exercising must become a habit. He adds, "As you age, you probably burn fewer calories so there can be a tendency to gain weight. EatingLess and exercising more is the answer."

"If you are ever going to play a game with him, be prepared toLose."

Judd Diefendorf (brother)

"He was good at any sport that involved a ball. He was a fantastic ping pong player. I don't think I ever beat him and I wasn't half bad myself."

DickLudlow (lifelong friend)

Evelyn's Interests: Music and Dancing

Evelyn's piano teacher was a fabulous pianist who played at her father's restaurant. She tookLessons for seven years, although when she got older she really didn't want to practice. She always wanted to play drums but her parents wouldn'tLet her. However, she has been known to play the bongos at parties.

Throughout herLife, Evelyn has always enjoyed dancing. "My grandfather was a great dancer and I used toLove to dance with him." Her brother was a very talented tap dancer and she danced with him in shows. Evelyn was also a drum majorette,Leading the Manhasset High School Band and Manhasset-Lakeville Firemen's Band. Additionally, there were many school dances where she danced—mostly the jitterbug or two-step to popular music of the time.

As she reflects, "I went to so many dances, both formal and informal, I can't even count them." She also enjoyed the music and dancing at her father's restaurants and even won a Charleston contest with Dick Van Dyke as her partner. After marriage, Evelyn and Dief used to host or attend fabulous theme and costume parties in Brookville where they would dance and sing and sometimes play charades.

> Dief: I wish I hadLearned how to do theLindy and dance better. My dancing school was too proper and weLearned too many formal dances. I've always regretted this.

Evelyn's Interests: Hobbies

Evelyn's parents nurtured in her an appreciation for art, music andLearning. SheLearned many handiworks from her mother and grandmother including sewing, crocheting and knitting. While in high school, she did volunteer work for the war effort by knitting sweaters for the Red Cross. When her children were young, she made clothes for them and always created their Halloween costumes.

She was also a real collector. Evelyn started collecting stamps, coins, and rocks at a young age. She remembers especiallyLiking to buy a particular type of firework called jackasses for the Fourth of July because in each package there was a Chinese coin. She has continued to maintain collections through the years and has interested her children and grandchildren in developing collections as well.

Evelyn has always been an avid reader and has fond memories of her mother reading to her. She really started reading, almost to excess, when she was eight and was hospitalized with pneumonia and bedridden for about six weeks. She read one book each day. She still is a voracious reader. SheLikes to tell children, "If you know how to read, you canLearn anything you want."

She keeps her mind active by doing crossword puzzles daily and playing bridge with friends. She also enjoys all types of arts and crafts but never seems to have enough time to work on them. After retirement she took up oil painting and finds that rainy days are good for this.

Evelyn muses, "I suppose you could call me 'a jack of all trades, master of none,' although I would rather be called 'well-rounded.'"

Evelyn's Interests: Sports

As a child, Evelyn enjoyed roller-skating, sledding, playing sports and games with her friends, and going to the beach to swim. She remembers "between the ages of four and eight, I only had boys to play with in our area. Since all the boysLiked my brother, they wouldLet me play with them and participate in their games." SheLearned to ride a bike about age six, roller skated from age five and sailed from age 12.

Evelyn andLee also went horseback riding and boating on their 36-foot Chris-Craft with their mother and father on Mondays, as her father worked weekends. In her teens, Evelyn preferred team sports, playing field hockey, soccer, basketball andLacrosse as she enjoyed the teamwork and the competition with other schools.

As an adult, she was an excellent bowler and competitive in tennis and golf. She also enjoys watching sporting events on TV. Her favorite sports team is the New York Yankees because it was her favorite when she was a kid and she is stillLoyal to her New York roots.

> Evelyn: Exercise and proper diet are most important, but even these can be overdone. I stand by the motto "everything in moderation," and think that some people are too fanatical and don't allow themselves to enjoy things that may not necessarily be good for them.

> I have always wanted toLearn how to fly. It always seemedLike such a thrilling and exciting thing to be able to soar through the air in a small plane. If I were healthy enough, I wouldn't mind going to outer space. I have always believed in space travel and that there wasLife on planets other than our own—maybe in a different galaxy.

Evelyn's Interests: Accounting

Evelyn was taught about money at an early age, opening her first personal savings account with her father when she was eleven. "The cashier must have hated me because I was often in the bank, sometimes to withdraw five cents for an ice cream cone." Evelyn also remembers sitting on her mother'sLap while she was doing the bookkeeping for the restaurant. When she got older, Evelyn did all of the bookkeeping and finances for her parent's restaurant whenever they were on a trip or away from home.

Evelyn formalized her bookkeeping, accounting, typing and shorthand skills at Mrs. Skinner's School. All through her marriedLife, she was responsible for family finances and was treasurer of many organizations. Evelyn obviously had a knack for numbers and took on many of these responsibilities because she was so capable, responsible and willing.

Shared Interests: Travel

Neither Evelyn nor Dief traveled abroad as children. At age 21, compliments of the U.S. Navy in WW II, Dief had the opportunity to travel around the Pacific. This instilled in Dief a taste for travel. He has taken much pleasure over the years planning and taking trips with Evelyn, his children and grandchildren, and also with a myriad of friends.

When Dief was 40 and Evelyn 35, they took their first trip to Europe with their children for six weeks.

They went to Spain, Italy, Switzerland, France, Belgium, and The Netherlands. While in Italy at Evelyn's father's birthplace in Borgofranco where he had restored an old family home, they had a big party to celebrate Dief's 40th birthday, complete with fireworks from the terrace across the frontLawn. They ended the vacation with a five-day voyage across the Atlantic on The Rotterdam. That was the first of many trips abroad that the Diefendorf's took as a family.

Since then and especially after retirement, Evelyn and Dief have traveled a great deal throughout the United States and around the world. Evelyn would stillLike to see St. Petersburg and take some more cruises, but at her age she says, "I'll be happy to go to the family home in Italy every year for a few weeks just to relax, enjoy the scenery and get together with our friends over there." Dief agrees that he wouldLike to go to Borgofranco annually for as many years as he is physically able. He describes it as "a great place to unwind, read and rest. No television, radio, or telephone. It's a dramatic change from our normalLife – a wonderful change of pace." Dief feels that he has seen most of what he'dLike to see in the world, but he is never at a shortage for ideas, withLingering thoughts about a cruise from Singapore around India and Africa or a trip to Finland andLeningrad.

Both Evelyn and Dief believe that there is no better way to get to know your family and create memories that you can share with your family in the future than through travel. Their family has always been a traveling family and this tradition has been handed down to their children and grandchildren. According to them, traveling is a wonderful way to gain an understanding of different cultures and toLearn to better appreciate your own home and country. Thoughtful travel adds a great deal of zest toLife.

Shared Interests: Church and Community

Throughout herLife, Evelyn volunteered for many civic and church activities. During the early 1960s, she was President of the Women's Guild at the Brookville Church, Vice President of the Consistory, was both a deacon and an elder, and was the treasurer and chairman of the finance committee. She was also a Sunday School teacher and sang in the church choir.

Additionally, she taught many classes for the Nassau County Extension Service of Cornell University. She was President of the PTA and a class mother for many years. She was also active in scouting, working with the Cub Scouts,Leading Girl Scouts for 10 years and serving as County Executive for Girl Scouts for two years. Most notably, she volunteered over 5,000 hours at the Glen Cove Community Hospital.

After retiring to Pinehurst, she was co-moderator and treasurer of the women's coordinating team, missionary chairman, and twice chairwoman of Circle #5 at the Community Presbyterian Church. She continues to be an active member of the Women's Republican Club and the English Speaking Union.

Dief proudly shares, "Whatever activity Evelyn became involved in she would rise to aLeadership position—whether it was the PTA, church work or club activities. You can also count on her to follow through and do a thorough job in any task she undertakes. If I were to write a book about her, I'd entitle it "A DependableLeader.""

Dief has also been active in church and community activities. As a young adult and a member of the Brookville Reformed Church, a friend asked him to substitute for his Sunday School class one week. Twenty yearsLater, Dief was still teaching Sunday School. Now that he is retired, he has more time to devote to church and civic affairs. At the Pinehurst Community Presbyterian Church, he is chairman of the church endowment committee and a church elder serving on the finance committee. He is on the scholarship committee of the Tin Whistles and a past president of the English Speaking Union.

What were the most dramatic changes in yourLifetime?

Dief:

Television – News is visual and immediate. It also provides us with sport events and entertainment. The only problem is that too many hours are spent watching TV.

Shopping – Since WWII, shopping centers have been built and have completely changed the shopping habits of Americans

Computer – No business can operate successfully without being computerized. Individuals are also finding the computer indispensable for communication through e-mail, record keeping, buying products, making travel arrangements, plus all types of information. All of these make a computer a must.

Evelyn:

Flying – Commercial flying has changed many of ourLives. We can go all over the world with ease now. Since we bothLove to travel, as do our children and grandchildren, we have much more opportunity to get to know different cultures.

TV – Television has also changed ourLives. Aside from the many programs on TV, we have instant news now. It used to be gleaned only from the newspaper, radio and the newsreels at the movies, and that was often atLeast a weekLate and sometimes biased.

Appliances – For women, the greatest changes have been the washing machine, then the dryer, and the dishwasher as well as wash and wear clothing. These changes have given women more time to play golf or tennis and pursue other hobbies. For working women these changes have also been a blessing.

Chapter Five
Life Lessons

Family values have always been very important to the Diefendorf and Broglio families. From early ages, Dief and Evelyn were both taught the importance of honesty and integrity, hard work and frugality, responsibility and dependability, and spirituality and faith. These characteristics were built into their every dayLives and have provided a strong foundation. They both inherited a good value system and as they grew older, it was almost second nature to care about people. Here they share someLessons they haveLearned and wouldLike to pass on to future generaticns.

LifeLesson #1: If you do the right thing, things will turn out right.

Evelyn: Maintaining high moral values and acting with integrity allows us to distinguish right from wrong and thereby makes decisions far easier. Although some decisions are difficult, both of us think that we know the right from the wrong and will follow the path of the "right." This makes us dependable, and people know where we stand. It also generallyLeads to mutual trust between us and the people with whom we are associated. We believe that being a ChristianLeads you to strong moral values that will dictate how youLead yourLife. Your upbringing has aLot to do with what you deem is right and wrong. Fortunately, our parents and grandparents were very ethical people.

Do unto others as you would have them do unto you.

Dief: I was faced with a business challenge in 1965. I had no one to talk to at the Home Office because the Vice President only spent time working with agencies with problems and mine was aLeading agency among the 200 sales offices in the company. So Evelyn was my consultant. I was really uncomfortable with a few of the people in our agency. I didn'tLike the way they conducted business. It wasn't our agency's style. I didn't quite trust them and I was thinking about asking them toLeave. EvelynListened to me and supported my judgment and my decision toLet some people go, in spite of the fact that I would beLosing about 30% of the agency's production. It was the gutsiest thing I had ever done. I did it, because it was the right thing to do although it was a very difficult decision. Some of my agents were quite critical of me and the home office couldn't believe what I had done. I explained to the Vice President that my agency wasLike a garden but it had weeds and in order to have a beautiful garden the weeds had to be removed. As time passed, our agency grew proving that my decision was correct. In my heart I knew I had made the right decision.

Here is some advice I gave Roey when he was starting out in business. He was sitting at his desk getting ready to make the first call of his career. I knocked at the door, popped my head around the corner and said, "I want you to remember one thing. If you do the right thing, you will never have to worry about money. Go get 'em." He decided toListen. As Roey now remarks, "After 34 years in business, there has never been a day in my career where this credo didn't work. The Diefendorf philosophy of business was passed from one generation to the next and has become part of my 'code of ethics.'"

Be honest with yourself and with those about you.

LifeLesson #2: Family comes first. Taking care of family is part of being a family.

Evelyn: My father instilled in us a desire to help other people. When my grandmother died, my father took care of many of my mother's siblings. Several of them came toLive with us and were raised as my siblings. My father supported some of them with jobs at his restaurant since jobs were hard to come by during the Depression. He did this willingly and graciously since they were part of our family.

Dief: The death of my father would have been more tragic for the family if he had not been such a wise and successful businessman. He was very responsible, and in spite of his dying in the midst of the Great Depression, he believed in the insurance business and had an insurance plan that could provide for us in the event of his premature death. Basically, the insurance benefit was what my mother used as an income to raise the three of us even though ourLives changed dramatically from what it was prior to my father's death. My father's foresight provided an income to my mother for the next 39 years until her death and enabled her toLive aLife of financial dignity. The first of each month, for over 39 years, a check arrived from MONY. It really was aLoveLetter that said, "I'm thinking of you and ILove you."

Above all, your family is most deserving of your thoughts and yourLove. They are the most important people in yourLife; treat them as such. You can provide direction to what your childrenLearn through family involvement. This includes family activities such as making sure the children do their homework, attending church together, taking family trips and showing a tangible interest in your children's activities. I could sum this up by saying that one of our family traditions was "togetherness." You get to know each other and you share new experiences that will be treasured memories over aLifetime.

LifeLesson #3: Dreams are what get you started. Discipline is what keeps you going.

Evelyn: The most important value imparted to me was the Broglio family work ethic. My father, Frank, was an immigrant who came to this country when he was eighteen and had to start from the bottom. My father personifies the American Dream. He began working as a busboy and eventually owned his own successful and highly regarded restaurants. He had a strong work ethic and workedLong hours, getting only about four hours of sleep a night. He believed that if you work hard and do good there will be noLimit to your success. He instilled in us a very good work ethic.

Dief: My mother, Catharine, was a hard worker who sacrificed for her three boys. To save money, she never used aLaundry service, but instead did her own washing, hung the clothes on a clothesline in the backyard, and then ironed them. She was very frugal. ILearned from that, and as I always explain, my two brothers and I ordered from the right side of the menu. We would see what was theLeast expensive meal and that's what we would order.

Hard work and discipline are important forLearning new skills. Here's a goodLesson: Mickey Mantle's sons wanted to play baseball so Mickey got them the batting audition. There was only one problem – they couldn't hit. So remember, it doesn't matter who your father, grandfather, or great grandfather was. You have toLearn how to hit. Having the name Diefendorf might get you the audition, but you have toLearn how to play the game! Do not trust inLuck to bring you success.

There is very LittleLuck in Life; you make your ownLuck.

To be financially successful you must be able to distinguish between needs and wants.

As for money, don't spend what you don't have or can't afford. Don'tLet your wants and desires overwhelm your needs. To succeed financially there is no substitute for the habit of saving. Money alone will not guarantee happiness; in fact, it may encourage greed, selfishness, materialism and self-centeredness—all of which bring on unhappiness. We believe that high moral values, ethical behavior, a good work ethic and a deep spiritual faith will sustain you throughoutLife and give you the strength to overcome any adversities you may face.

LifeLesson #4: Making your children responsible for their ownLives will build their independence as well as their dependability.

Dief: We all had household chores for which we were responsible. My chores were to set the table and dry the dishes and put them away after my older brother,

Warren, washed them. I was also responsible for taking out the garbage. At times, I would wash and simonize the car, cut the grass and shovel snow. I didn't get an allowance but my mother would pay me for big jobs such as putting up and taking down huge storm windows for the front porch that were stored across the street in my grandfather's garage. Additionally, I helped the church's sexton,Louis Caputo, with church chores so that my friends and I could use the church's basketball court.

As part of a family, you do your share of the work. I don't remember exactly what our children did around the house, but during high school and college they got summer jobs on their own to earn spending money. It is best not to spoil children with too much help.

Evelyn: I did not get an allowance. I used to earn money in other ways, such as posing for my mother's art class,Leading the firemen's band and writing a society news column for theLocal newspaper. I cashiered at my father's restaurant during summer vacations when I was in high school. I don't remember how much I made, but it must have been satisfactory because I always had enough money to buy Christmas and birthday gifts for my family and to bank some money as well.

At home, I helped my mother,Lillian, by washing the dishes while she dried them. I also helped with the cleaning in the summer so that the family could get to the beach sooner. Other than that, my only real responsibilities were to do my schoolwork, practice the piano, and clean my room. We just had to help out in anyway we could. We required about the same amount of cooperation from our children.

It's important to encourage your children's independence andLet themLearn from their own experience. Telling my children about all of my mistakes wouldn't do much good. When I made any decisions, I thought they were the right things to do at the time. It would make me too unhappy to go back and rehash all the things I may have done wrong. It would beLike beating a dead horse. If my children or grandchildren need advice from me, they can ask for it any time. Hopefully, they have as much knowledge as they need to make their own choices.

Try to set a good example for your children, grandchildren and for the people who work with you.

LifeLesson #5: Your attitude determines your altitude, that is, just how high you'll go in yourLifetime.

Dief:Life is 10% what happens to you and 90% how you react to it. Everyone in hisLifetime gets some good breaks and some bad breaks. We tend to take the good breaks in stride, but those so-called bad breaks can really get us down. How do you react to bad breaks? Your attitude makes all the difference. Adversity can build character, build internal strength; it brings out the best in people.

Are you positive or negative, do you see the good in things or the bad, do you see opportunities or roadblocks, do you make people feel happy by the way you act, do you smile or frown, do you find the good in people or do you find the faults in people? Your attitude is of utmost importance for your success and happiness.

Don't be too cynical or you'll end up an unhappy person.

ALong time ago someone told me about the KASH formula: K stands for knowledge; A stands for attitude; S stands for skills; and H stands for habits. Some parts of it are more important than others. Of these four parts, which do you think is most important? Which is theLeast important?

Attitude is the most important. Obviously, there are positive attitudes and negative attitudes. More simply put: if you think you can, you can; if you think you can't, you won't even try.

Using tennis as an illustration,Let's apply the KASH formula. First, you have to have a positive attitude about tennis to put a racket in your hand and go out on the court and hit a ball, otherwise you would probably never attempt to play. If the next step is to try to improve your game you must develop the habit of practice. In addition to the habit of practice you now need instruction toLearn how to hold the racket, strike the ball, hit a serve, etc. In other words you are now increasing your knowledge and improving your tennis skills. If you don't want to get better (attitude) and don't practice (habits), then no matter how much knowledge of tennis you have you will not be a skilled player. This sequence of relationships between attitudes, habits, knowledge and skills is applicable to everything you do inLife.

From good attitudes come good habits. Both are action oriented. It is important to be a creature of habit so we don't have to think consciously about our every action. People possessing both of these traits get right to the job at hand and finish it. They are notLikely to procrastinate which is a big time waster and one of the biggest causes of failure. It is also best not to worry about things over which you have no control.

Our grandchildren know about the KASH formula. I wrote aLetter to them several years ago asking them to rank the importance of the four parts and to send me their answers. I then compiled their responses and reported back to them. Their responses were very thoughtful and I was pleased to see that they had rated attitude as their top choice.

LifeLesson #6: Accentuate the positive and watch out for the negative.

Evelyn: Take each day as it comes; do the best that you can and accentuate the positive in everything that you do. This way, most things will work out well, and even some bad things may end up working for the best if you just keep the faith. With a positive attitude, some things that seem to be disasters when they happen, inLater years seem to be quite humorous. Roll with the punches, since everything doesn't always go off without a hitch. When traveling, try to take everything in as through the eyes of a child and you will be awed and enchanted by the experiences.

Dief: I am a firm believer that all things eventually turn out for the best. For instance, the death of my father was a tragedy for the family. This was a terrible blow to myLife and it changed ourLives dramatically. However, due to the events, I attended Stony Brook with the help of a substantial scholarship, metLee Broglio, was introduced to his sister, Evelyn, which eventuallyLed to my marriage to her and the birth of two children and six wonderful grandchildren. Ironically, if my father had not died, I would not have had theLife I have today with Evelyn, Martha, Roey, and our six grandchildren. I think my father's positive attitude influenced my outlook onLife and how I coped with the vicissitudes ofLife.

I have read all sorts of positive and inspirational books, such as Victor Frankel's "The Search for Meaning." The impact of many positive books also influenced myLife. Similarly, I have always tried to associate and surround myself with positive thinkers—what I call "can and will do" people. You can train yourself to be positive by reading positive books and surrounding yourself with positive thinkers. You can turn on the creative juices by "possibility thinking"—thinking about a better way to accomplish your objective.

Books that give a positive slant onLife

- PsychoCybernetics by Maxwell Maltz
- Loving Each Other byLeo Buscaglia
- The Power of Positive Thinking by Norman Vincent Peale
- Learned Optimism by Martin Seligman
- Acres of Diamonds by Russell Cornwell
- As a Man Thinketh by James Allen

Be positive, use possibility thinking; thisLeads to creativity.

A positive attitude causes people to be action oriented. These peopleLook to the future with enthusiasm because they expect good things to happen. They are imaginative and are the ones who make discoveries. They are receptive to new ideas and see opportunities. They are willing to take calculated risks. TheyLook on the bright side ofLife. They are fun to be with and are more concerned with opportunities than problems. It is also a fact they recover faster from illnesses.

Take Life seriously, but not yourself too seriously.

People with negative attitudes are not fun to be with and aren't very popular. They kill a good idea before it gets off the ground. They immediately tell you what's wrong or why something won't work. They are not responsible for much progress. People with negative attitudes don't work as hard or work as smart as those with a positive attitude. Generally the most negative people are professionals who have been taught to be analytical and explore what's wrong with a given proposition. Progress is never made by negative thinking. However, we must temper positive thinking with realism.

When we would discuss a new idea in my office, I would always preface the discussion by saying, "remember the wheelbarrow." This refers to an exercise that demonstrates the way most people react to a new idea by telling you why the idea is no good or won't work.

An audience is asked toLook at and comment on an illogically designed wheelbarrow. Generally, most comments given by adults are critical and point out the flaws. Anyone with any positive comments is so intimidated that he will not even speak up. Interestingly, when children around 10-12 years old are shown the design, they tend to find something good or atLeast neutral to say.

The moral to this exercise is that before an idea is killed by negative thoughts, all the positives should be explored first. In addition, people should consider the interesting things about the idea. Interesting reactions are more creative than critical ones.

LifeLesson #7: People are more important than possessions.
Love people. Use things. Not vice versa.

Dief: What isLife without friends? Without friendsLife isLonely.Life is all about people. Maintaining friendships demonstrates an interest in other people and keeps you from being too introspective. Friendships are good for your mental and physical health.

I have maintained friendships from all phases of myLife, even my childhood. On my first day of school, I remember a boy I met named DickLudlow. We maintained a strong friendship for 75 years. I make a conscious effort to keep in touch with old friends. As our friends onLong Island aged, moved from the community or passed away, we consciously sought out younger friends to replace those we hadLost. InLife it is important to continuously make new friendships, but never forget your old friends.

You'll be remembered more for your character than for what possessions youLeave.

Remember that developing friendships is more important than acquiring possessions. Possessions do not bring you true happiness nor is there anything truly enduring about them. Fifty years from now, our personal possessions will not be very meaningful. People who are possession obsessed can beLacking in people interest. What really counts is the quality of your personal relationships. They canLead to happiness and success rather than aLife of misery andLoneliness. Developing strong personal relationships is the key to a meaningful and successfulLife. Just how do you develop strong personal relationships? It happens when you thinkLess about yourself and more about others— your relatives, friends and acquaintances. Self-centered people are seldom happy people. Other-centered people enjoy the thrill of giving of themselves and of sharing.

Be other-centered rather than self-centered.
You have to work on this daily.

Here is an example from my work that demonstrates the difference between the importance of people versus a focus on money. As I entered into my final year as a General Sales Manager of a financial service office, my replacement, a sales vice-president of the company, overlapped thatLast year with me. I thought it would be advisable for him to know as much as possible about our 28 sales representatives. To accomplish this IListed each sales rep by name and gave as much information about each one as I could so my successor would have a greater understanding of each person. This included his family history, markets in which he worked, how to work with the representative effectively, his strengths and his shortcomings and in general how we helped our sales force achieve better production and equally important, how we encouraged him to use his talents in his community and other outside activities. After I had reviewed the first two sales persons, my successor stopped me cold and said he wasn't interested inLearning more but wanted to know what my over-rides were on each one. Over-rides are what determined my income. I told him I didn't know and he told me I wasn't a very good businessman if I didn't know, to which I replied, "If I can help these people become more successful in their businessLives as well as their personalLives then I will be well rewarded financially. And I'm really not concerned with how much I earn on the production of each salesperson." At this point I knew that this man would notLast veryLong. He didn't! He put money or himself first (I call these people the greed breed) whereas he should have put caring about these people first and money second. I often have said, "I am nothing without my sales people but I am everything with them."

Tony Campolo, a minister and inspirational speaker talks about titles or testimonies. How important are the titles you acquire over yourLifetime? They go to the grave with you. And, how important is the wealth you have acquired unless it is used for worthy purposes? However, testimonies areLasting, they come from people you have encouraged, given solace to, have inspired and helped alongLife'sLong and sometimes rough road. Friendships are not bought; they are earned by thoughtfulness.

Evelyn: A final note on relationships – be a good sounding board.Listen more and talkLess.Listening is an art; it must beLearnedListeningLeads to empathy. Until you walk in the other person's shoes you cannot fully understand the other person. It's more pleasant to be with a goodListener and someone who asks good questions than it is to be with a talker. When you talk, you say what you know or think you know, but when youListen youLearn what the other person is thinking. Be sincerely interested in what the other person has to say. You will find that almost everyone is very interesting if you take the time to get to know them. You may also be one of the few people he can talk to and express his innermost concerns. This is a true friend.

LifeLesson #8: We are better together; it takes an orchestra to play a symphony.

Evelyn: As with sports, I think working well with others requires teamwork. Naturally, if you're good at something, peopleLook to you forLeadership. You just have to be careful not to be too bossy and to use some tact with other peoples' shortcomings. Remember, in sports the one who assists in a play is just as important as the one who scores.

Marriage also requires aLot of team work. It is important to maintain your individuality and your uniqueness, but working out problems and solutions as a team is even more important.

You are never too old toLearn about working well with others. When I was 60 years old, we went for a week to New Mexico for a program calledLEAP (Leadership Experiential Adventure Program) which isLike an Outward Bound experience. It was a jam-packed week of different experiences to do as a team and to show how with teamwork and cheering each other on, you could accomplish things you never thought possible. The gutsiest thing I ever did physically was to dive off a cliff 350 feet high on a guide wire crossing the Pecos River, where members of my team were there on the other side to catch and unhook me, to cheer for me and hug me. Quite an adventure!

> It's better to have trust and faith in people and be hurt or disappointed by them than to have no trust or faith.

LifeLesson #9: Be kind to your spouse for aLasting marriage.

Evelyn: We enjoy many activities together, such as playing golf and travelling. But you don't always have to be "doing" something together for it to be a special time. Sometimes just sitting around and doing nothing, or quiet times when we are both reading are the most special. It's just nice to know that you have someone youLove to share your time with.

> *Principles for maintaining a healthy marriage (Evelyn):*

Naturally you have to be attracted to each other. I think it's best when you share the same beliefs and values. A husband and wife should be a team, and work together and talk together about all aspects of theirLives. They should discuss their dreams and goals for the future and both should know everything about their financial situation. If they have children, both should be involved with their children's education and activities. Also, always try toLook on the bright side of things or events. A good sense of humor is also essential.

Dief: The greater the compatibility between husband and wife, the greater theLikelihood of aLong and successful marriage. You must have respect for each other and you must be kind to each other. Whenever I pass through a receivingLine at a wedding I always tell the bride and groom, "Be kind to each other." Sometimes in myLife I was overly involved with my career to the detriment of being as thoughtful to my wife as I should have been.

Principles for maintaining a healthy marriage (Dief):

1) Have the same values
2) Have a strong religious belief, attend church and participate in church activities
3) Agree over major issues

4) Have a tendency toLike the same kind of people

5) Develop mutually exclusive interests and hobbies – have an independentLife

6) Have and pursue mutual interests – travel, golf, tennis, bridge, how to raise children, etc.

7) Don't squabble over money issues – don't spend money when you don't have it

8) Be completely faithful to each other

LifeLesson #10: Giving and helping others brings great joy and satisfaction.

Dief: Through our upbringing we had been taught to serve others and to be charitable. For instance, my grandfather gave a substantial gift at his death for the construction of a parish hall at the Chester Hill Methodist Church. Evelyn's parents were also very charitable. Serving and giving came naturally and has been a way ofLife for us.

My greatest enjoyment inLife is to think about and help someone or to write out aLarge check to a worthwhile causeLike the Stony Brook School. For me, my contributions to the Stony Brook School are a way of repaying them and thanking them for the financial aid they gave my brothers and me. It pleases me greatly to have set up the Catharine Diefendorf Scholarship Fund with my brothers at the time of our mother's death. Later my wife and I established the Evelyn and Monroe Diefendorf Faculty Educational Fund at the school. Additionally, I co-chaired the first major fund raising campaign for the Stony Brook School in 2001, surpassing the $7 million goal and raising $8.9 million. This was a partial payback for the generous scholarships that my two brothers and I received to attend the school. For the most part, we have concentrated our philanthropic efforts in the field of education.

A few years ago, we gave each of our six grandchildren $50 in early November which they had to give away before Christmas. Evelyn and I were greatly pleased by the thoughtfulness of each grandchild in his or her selection. We feel that each of them smelled the sweet aroma that comes from the joy of giving.

To round out yourLives, make sure you acquire the habit of generosity. This includes giving of your time and talents as well as your money. The most worthwhileLives are those that unselfishly give of themselves to their families, their church and to the community atLarge.

Evelyn: Of course, it was natural to help our children to get a head start onLife. We provided our children with the finest education available, helped with the purchase of their first homes, and contributed to our grandchildren's education. In addition to the funds for

Stony Brook, we also created the Evelyn and Monroe Diefendorf Scholarship Fund at our church and the Frank andLillian Broglio Annual Merit Award given to a member of the Borgofranco Filamonica. As education is important to us, we also have been actively involved in providing four annual and renewable scholarships through the Tin Whistle organization in Pinehurst.

I really don't go out of my way to help the needy, although I do thingsLike bringing Thanksgiving dinner to a needy family; bringing food and clothing to the Coalition for Human Care; bringing clothing and toiletries to the shelter for abused women & unwed mothers; giving scholarships to needy children; contributing to the minister's discretionary fund forLocal emergency help; supplying blankets and food for emergency relief; doing Christmas packages for poorer children. We do all of these things and more. I think the recipients are all very appreciative of our efforts and it makes us feel good about ourselves to do this. The joy is internal not external.

Be charitable.

LifeLesson # 11: Sharing your insights helps others succeed.

Dief: A mentor is a wise and trusted counselor. I haveLearned a great deal from people I have met during myLifetime and hopefully acquired some of their wisdom. In turn, I have tried to share my wisdom and insights with my children, grandchildren, business associates or others who have crossed myLife. My whole businessLife was devoted to helping people do better, not only in business but also in their personalLives.

Just thinking about someone else indicates that you care about this person. Putting these thoughts into action shows that you are sincerely interested in his or her welfare which I guess proves the old adage that "Actions speakLouder than words." The motivation for mentoring and helping someone to be the best that they can be is watching their growth. All I need in return from these people is a simple "Thank you." My files are full ofLetters from people I have helped. After being retired for almost 20 years I continue to receive thank youLetters from my agency associates with whom I've had a deep andLasting relationship. To me, this is my ultimate payoff inLife.

From a business perspective, mentoring can be much more efficient, successful andLess costly than training programs.Learning from an established professional reduces turnover and gives the new recruit or employee a better chance to succeed. My advice to a novice is: don't try to make it on your own when a proven road map is available.

I consider helping someone to succeed or influencing someone in a positive way as a personal success for myself as well. I get satisfaction from the personal acceptance and personal recognition it brings me although it is important not to diminish the accomplishments of those we have helped by taking too much credit. My suggestion for older folks is, if you want to feel young and think young, try mentoring. It's good for your mental and physical health.

In the final analysis, have I had a positive impact on others'Lives?Let me add, it's not the number ofLives that's so important, but is even just one person a better person because of myLife on this earth?

Your ultimate success will be measured by theLives you have touched in a positive way.

In aLetter to his father Roey wrote, *"There's just no way I could say thank you for all that you have done for me. Through all the years while I was growing up, to now, you have shared so much with me. TheLove of people, theLove of God, and theLove of family are some of the things that come to mind first. You have given me opportunities that few have had; providing me with an education that could not have been topped, fun and adventure that could not have been duplicated and friendship of which no friend could ask for more."*

LifeLesson #12: Building a home court advantage has a positive influence on others'Lives.

Dief: In sports, teams tend to win more games while playing at home than while playing on the opponent's field. Put simply, they play better because of the support of the home crowd. After retirement, I was reflecting on the success of my agency and it came to me that we had build a home court advantage during the years I had the privilege of being sales manager. We had given our people a positive environment in which to grow and encouraged continued education. Frequently, I could see in people talents that they could not see in themselves. As sales manager, I was the equivalent of the cheering crowd encouraging the players to excel.

I firmly believe that parents can build a home court advantage for their children and grandchildrenLeading them to accomplishments greater than they might have reached under normal circumstances. In essence, the parents are the cheerleaders. Hopefully, Evelyn and I have demonstrated by our actions our interest in our children and grandchildren and have had a positive influence on theirLives. Throughout myLife I have written positive notes to my children and grandchildren as well as my associates. ILove thinking about people and everyoneLikes encouragement or a pat on the back.

In addition to positive reinforcement, I am a firm believer in incentives. Here are a few examples of how I have used incentives in my personalLife. I had a group of boys ages 10-12 in my Sunday School class. Each week they would get points for attendance and for passing a test on that Sunday'sLesson. If they accumulated enough points, and most of them did, I would take them to a Mets or Yankee baseball game or a hockey game. Evelyn said I was bribing these kids, but I thought of it as an incentive to participate and do well.

When my son, Roey, was just in high school he decided he wanted to sell insurance during the summer. I told him I would give him S5 for every person he asked to buy. He was very imaginative and one day he had made aList of the MONY trustees to phone for an appointment. He actually reached some of them and amazingly, some of them bought insurance for their children and grandchildren. At the end of six weeks, he had earned $1,500 in commissions besides what I had given him. We always had an incentive orLittle deal going on.

I knew my grandson, Steven, didn'tLike to read due to his dyslexia so I decided to make a deal with him one summer. I told him that for every book he read, I would give him $5. Being an honest young man, he suggested that the books shouldn't be too short or have too many pictures. ILooked over at his older sister, Katie, and could see her pouting, mostLikely because she wasn't included in the deal. So I quickly told her I wasn't finished yet and offered her $5 for every book she read. Then Steven became sullen because he knew Katie was a very fast reader. I was scrambling as I went along, not wanting to discourage either one and wanting to make things fair. I said, "Now, Steven, for every book Katie reads, you get $5; and Katie, for every book Steven reads, you get $5." They were both quite excited. By the time of the big pay-off in September and in spite of many other summer activities, they had each read nine books. Steven calculated the amount I owed them very quickly, telling me "Poppy, I'm fast with numbers. Put a dollar sign in front and I'm even faster." We had the same arrangement the following summer. By the end of the second year, Steven had acquired the habit of reading and we also had some fun along the way. Katie had already been a good reader but she had encouraged her brother to continue reading. This summer program provided a feeling of camaraderie between the children as they both encouraged each other to read.

LifeLesson #13: Know who you are and where you are going, then be proactive.

Dief: How many people think and plan theirLives? Do they set goals for themselves? Are most people drifters? Are they in command of theirLives or are theirLives dictated by outside forces? Are they pro-active or re-active?

I developed an Annual Goals Folder that I used for myself and with the people who worked with me. Every year, each person would set goals for personal improvement, both for business andLong-range plans. At the end of the year, we would reflect cn progress and determine goals for the new year. This meant that people were willing to be evaluated. It would help them know themselves better, know their capabilities, and keep them fromLiving in a dream world. It helped them excel in their present work which is mandatory for having a brilliant future.

It is good to set goals for yourself in order to be in command of yourLife. It is also good to take stock of who you are. A philosophical friend of mine told me, "The older you get, the more you become the kind of person you really are." For example, if you are kind, you become kinder; if you are miserly, you become more miserly. TheLesson is: Take stock of yourself today and get to know who you are so you'll know what you'll beLike in the future. If you recognize your shortcomings, remember they'll be magnified as you get older. You can take steps today to change the direction of the characteristics that will dominate yourLife. Additionally, associate with people you wouldLike to beLike and you'll beLike them. ILearned that if you don't surround yourself with really top-notch people you cannot be top-notch.

Every day when I wake up, I don't say, "What am I going to do today?" ILook at the To DoList that I made up the previous night and I start the day running. You not only need to set goals for yourself, but you also need to take action to achieve them.

It is important to be careful of your ultimate career goal. For example, I was tempted to make a run for the position of Executive Vice President of MONY that might haveLed to the presidency. Titles are tempting but fleeting. There is always plenty of potential in your present job when you are in a position that is measured by your personal excellence. Testimonies for your achievement and competency are forever.

Your worth is more important than your wealth.

LifeLesson #14: Stay focused on doing the important things first.

Evelyn: I have always been fairly well organized. Even as a young student I used to do my homework in the same order as my class schedule, so that the same amount of time had elapsed in between class hours and homework time.Later on, I would tackle the hardest thing first.

Dief: Too often people don't get to the heart of the matter. They have a tendency to skirt around the edge of the problem or situation. Simply put, they don't focus. They get involved in aLot of trivia and don't focus on what is important. The small picture overwhelms theLarge picture. The key to success is doing the important things first.

Get to the heart of the matter.

When you pack the trunk of a car do you put theLarge suitcases in first or do you put in all the small packages first? Think about which you do and why. Obviously, theLarge ones must go in first if you want to fit everything in. So remember, tackle the big things first.

Evelyn: Here is a story ILike about setting priorities:

A philosophy professor had some items in front of him. When the class began, wordlessly, he picked up a veryLarge and empty mayonnaise jar and proceeded to fill it with golf balls. He then asked the students if the jar was full. They agreed that it was.

So the professor then picked up a box of pebbles and poured them into the jar. He shook the jarLightly. The pebbles rolled into the open areas between the golf balls. He then asked the students again if the jar was full. They agreed it was.

The professor next picked up a box of sand and poured it into the jar. Of course, the sand filled up everything else. He asked once more if the jar was full. The students responded with a unanimous "yes."

The professor then produced two cups of coffee from under the table and poured the entire contents into the jar, effectively filling the empty space between the sand. The studentsLaughed. As theLaughter subsided, the professor said, "I want you to recognize that this jar represents yourLife. The golf balls are the important things—family, children, health, friends and your favorite passions—things that if everything else wasLost and only they remained, yourLife would still be full. The pebbles are the other things that matter,Like your job, your house and your car. The sand is everything else—the small stuff.

"If you put the sand into the jar first," he continued, "there is no room for the pebbles or the golf balls. The same goes forLife. If you spend all your time and energy on the small stuff, you will never have room for the things that are important to you. Pay attention to the things that are critical to your happiness, the things that really matter. Play with your children. Take time to get medical checkups. Take your spouse out to dinner. Play another 18. There will always be time to clean the house and fix the disposal." Set your priorities. The rest is just sand."

One of the students raised her hand and inquired what the coffee represented. The professor smiled. "I'm glad you asked. It just goes to show you that no matter how full yourLife may seem, there's always room for a couple of cups of coffee with a friend."

LifeLesson #15: Research and planning help in making good decisions.

Evelyn: Decisions are frequently made with tooLittle thought. Sometimes people fly by the seat of their pants without considering the consequences. Dief and ILike to use the proverbial yellow pad with aLine down the middle for positives and negatives. This has helped us to make many decisions such as selecting new cars as well as buying the house in Pinehurst.

It is just as important to be organized and carefully plan what you want to do. For example, I drew up the specs for our home in Brookville. We also had a blueprint for our "financial" home. We planned our investments and finances andLived according to budgets we set for ourselves. Dief, always one to prepare, began thinking about retirement well beforehand by reading books on retirement and putting ideas into his "retirement file." As he would say, preparing for retirement isLike preparing for a new career.

Dief's "Tips for Retirement"

• Read books written about retirement.

- Talk to retired people andListen to their suggestions.
- Start a file at age 50 in which you store any idea or project that may be of interest to you after your retirement.
- Get a head start on those things you wouldLike to do after retiring. If you wouldLike to paint after you retire, start taking paintingLessons prior to retirement.
- Develop interests in organizations in which you can use your talents.

Dief says heLearned to think and to get organized while working in the Marketing and Development Division for 18 months under Homer Wood. This is where he claims he got his Ph.D. in thinking. What heLearned was tremendously helpful to him in his management career. One thing he did annually was to hold a two-day management meeting to plan out the coming year's activities. That way, the work plan was organized and everyone could plan their personal activities to coincide with the agency's plans.

Planning and being organized was also helpful in other areas ofLife as well. Perhaps one of the best examples is how we approached preparing for a trip. We would always buy books to get information about the area we were going to visit and talk to people who were knowledgeable about the area to give us a good idea of what we'dLike to do and see. Then Dief would make up a daily chart of activities with tours, restaurants and other points of interest. If we were going to a country where we didn't speak theLanguage, I would try toLearn a few words. I think the care Dief put into planning trips was why our friendsLiked to travel with us.

LifeLesson #16: Your mind will stay alive if you keep it turned on.

Dief: Never stopLearning! Be interested inLearning throughout your wholeLife, whether it is formal or informal education. For instance, Evelyn received aLife InsuranceLicense and Health InsuranceLicense and passed the ten exams necessary to receive the CLU designation in theLate '60s. Roey earned the following designations: Monroe M. Diefendorf, Jr., MI, CLU, ChFC, CFP, RFC, CIMA. He took my words to heart when I told him that the only replacement for education is ignorance.

Being involved and using your imagination keeps your mind alive and yourLife vibrant. Imagination played a part in my businessLife. I brought in speakers, conducted/organized innovative programs and training sessions, hosted the annual picnic and the agency dinner. The result was that the agency had an excellent spirit and we had a stimulating office to work in.

It is said that the brain is a muscle and that if you use it you areLessLikely to get Alzheimer's. Imagination results from possibility thinking—thinking outside the box. It results from positive thinking, not negative thinking. It adds excitement to your organization, not to mention excitement to yourLife. Imagination is also energized by thinking of others rather than yourself.

Most people uponLeaving their office at 5 p.m. switch the button to off and do not think about their work. If you are strictly an employee, this may work out just fine. However, if you are an entrepreneur, a business owner or someone who is compensated for his productive accomplishment, you will be in trouble if your mind closes down at 5 p.m.

One of the most creative times for the mind is at night when your subconscious is working. You canLet your mind work while you rest and get an advantage on your competition. ILike to record my creative ideas as they occur during the night. I keep a pad of paper and a special pen with a built-inLight next to the bed. I sometimes even get up in the middle of the night and type up notes or memos on the computer. I also find that my mind is active while I'm driving. Again, so as not toLose my ideas, I have a pencil and note paper next to me on the driver's side on which I can record my thoughts.

Evelyn is a morning person and does her best thinking in the morning. She does concede, however, that one's mind continues working during sleep. Many times after having gone to bed with a problem on her mind, she arises with the solution.

LifeLesson #17: Don't be afraid to yell "help!"

Dief: Most people go it alone and do not ask for help. One of the things I found out is that if you ask, people will be anxious to assist. ILearned this many years ago when I was building an office from scratch as a sales manager. Immediately, I sought out the advice of five of the top sales managers in New York City who worked for the best companies in the industry. I was actually amazed that they all agreed to meet with me. These men, the best in the country, were very generous with their time and gave me good advice.

Another time, I asked MONY's #1 manager, Dick Myer, who was about to retire, if I could visit with him. I knew he could help me. I spent two days with himLearning how he became so successful. I benefited because it opened my eyes to many new ideas. He was not only pleased to assist me, but he was also touched by my interest in him and my desire toLearn. At the end of the second day, he called our Home Office and said he had found his successor. This was my big break in business.

Another way of getting help is through study groups. When you get together with people who have similar interests or problems, everyoneLearns and benefits. I have participated in many study groups, most notably:

- Research Agencies Group (RAG) – a group of 20 managers from various companies from across the country who met twice a year at which time four research papers were delivered and then published in national journals. These people represented the cream of the business and ILearned as much from them in informal discussions as I did in more formal discussions.
- The Roundtable of New York City – a group of 30 sales managers from different companies who met each month to share their knowledge and expertise.
- The Pacesetter Group – a group of MONY managers who met twice a year to discuss areas of mutual interest.

- Informal group – five of us in NYC from different companies who became close friends and would meet for breakfast orLunch a few times each year.

I alsoLearned by attending seminars, conferences and meetings, through interactions with professors, management consultants and industryLeaders, and by avidly reading books relating to my profession. I found that books on psychology gave me a greater understanding of human nature.

LifeLesson #18: There IS power in prayer.

Evelyn: My belief in prayer has always been strong. I never pray for frivolous things – only for the well-being of family, my friends and me. I pray for God to give me the guidance to make the right decisions or to take the right actions.

I contracted pneumonia when I was about eight years old. I had a temperature of 108° and was not expected toLive. Every night, the whole crew of about 30 men who worked for my father would hold a prayer meeting and say the Rosary for me. When I wasLater told about this, it made me a true believer in prayer and its power.

God has answered many prayers for me. Here are a few examples:

1) When my brother was in the service during WWII as an army pilot, I prayed for him to come home safely.

2) When our first granddaughter was born, she was premature and needed all of our prayers, as did her mother, Chris, who had developed acute toxemia. Our prayers were answered. Ashley is perfect and Chris had three more wonderful daughters.

3) When our son Roey was young, he was very active, and as a result, had many accidents in sports or otherwise. It seems I said aLot of prayers in emergency rooms or on the way to get him whenever he had been hurt.

4) My husband has had several operations over the years, some of them quite serious. I'm sure that prayers helped pull him through successfully.

5) Our nephew, Frank, had a terrible automobile accident right before his graduation from high school. It was touch and go whether he would survive and I know all of our prayers helped pull him through.

A few years ago I had a frightening experience. When I was in the hospital, the machine that registered my vital signs went into a straightLine, and nurses came rushing in to help bring me back toLife. All I can remember is thinking, what a ridiculous way to die, and I started taking deep breaths. I was watching the machine and it started functioning again, and I thanked God for giving me another chance. Now, I probably would wish that I had cleaned all my closets before going to the hospital.

Through research it has been proven that prayer does help.

Dief: Prayer has played an important part in myLife. My prayers most often are prayers of thanksgiving. Studies tell us that praying helps. In some mystic way prayers are transmitted to the one in need and they have a positive effect.

MyLife has been rather free from serious setbacks or unpleasant experiences. My prayers are usually prayers of thanks. Every morning on my train commute to New York City I would say a prayer of thanks for all the good fortune that I've had in myLife.

Evelyn has had some medical setbacks over the past several years and I have prayed for her health. She was very sick with pneumonia and in intensive care for quite a few days. I prayed and prayed for her recovery. To the extent that she is doing quite well at this time, my prayers have been answered.

LifeLesson #19: Belief in God takes the fear out ofLife and the fear out of death.

Dief: Most important in ourLives is our faith in God. OurLives are in God's hands which means we do not fear the unknown or fear the future. We believe in the forgiveness of our sins through Jesus' death on the cross. Some things inLife you accept on faith; there doesn't actually have to be any proof, such as heaven. The acceptance that there is a heaven surely makes ourLife on earth more bearable and turns death into a celebration. We do not fear death since we know that in the future we will all be together again.

Many people seem to be more demonstrative and vocal about their Christianity than I am. Right or wrong, I feel my actions are more important than my words, and my actions will more clearly demonstrate my Christian beliefs.

Evelyn: My ideas about God have not changed much from when I was young. I have always felt that he is aLoving God, and that he made us in his own image. Therefore we all carry aLittle bit of God within us and this is our soul. Maybe God wasLeading me when I volunteered to do so many different things. However, good works cannot save you. Only the Grace of God can save you. If you feel that you have been blessed by the Grace of God, you will be happy to do good works. I think that following the Ten Commandments just about says it all.

LifeLesson #20: Give thanks for your good fortune of being born in America.

Dief: Almost 300 years ago in the early 1700s, the Diefendorf, Mechling and Monroe families immigrated to America some 60 years before the United States was born. The two reasons forLeaving Europe were persecution and opportunity. Even an agrarian economy was a welcome home for these new arrivals to America. When the War for Independence started, there were many members from all three families in the Colonial army fighting for independence from England. Today there is an organization called the Sons of the Revolution, in which I am a member, that accepts members who can establish through the family tree that there were family members who actually fought in the war.

During the Civil War all three families had members in the Union Army fighting to keep our nation united. On the Monroe side of the family we believe there were some men who fought with the Confederate Army. As bad as war is, both WW I and WW II closed the rift that had existed between North and South in our country as members of all the armed forces were thrown together andLearned toLive together and respect each other.

World War I found my father, Warren E. Diefendorf, a member of the 77th Division in France, in the thick of action. World War II came and once again members of our family enlisted to fight for our country and keep our country theLand of freedom and opportunity. I was in the Navy on an aircraft carrier in the Pacific, while my brother, Warren, was in the army seeing action in France and Germany.

Freedom and opportunity are the hallmarks of why people want to immigrate to the United States. And so it was with Evelyn's father, Frank Broglio, whoLiterately came to our country just after WWI withLittle money in his pocket but who had a vision of making a success of himself through hard work and taking advantage of the opportunities offered to individuals through the free enterprise system. He was able to avail himself of the freedom and opportunities in our country that other members of the family had so valiantly fought for. His success isLegendary and represents what is commonly named "Only in America".

Be worthy of your heritage. (Motto of Deerfield Academy)

The same reasons for attracting people from all over the world to our shores remain from the 1600s to today. Sometimes being born into the affluence of United States makes our natives oblivious to the price that has been paid by families for almost 400 years and in the case of our family for 300 years. I hope that our family will frequently reflect more on the country's attributes rather than its shortcomings and give thanks to their good fortune of being born in America.

LifeLesson #21:Less government is better than more government.

Evelyn: Politically, I am a moderate Republican. I have always been a Republican. I guess I must have been influenced by my parents and also my husband, but I have always believed that the government should not interfere with things that can be handled by the private sector.

Dief: I am aLiberal conservative—conservative to the extent that I believeLess government is better than more government. Discrimination is wrong and that includes affirmative action which is discriminatory. I believe in tax reductions to stimulate the economy rather than using government spending to stimulate the economy. I believe in capitalism and a free economy which have made our country the most humanitarian country on earth. My family initially influenced me and then by reading and study my native intelligence hasLed me to conservatism. My wife and I are pleased to fund a scholarship that invariably is given to a minority student. When I feel something is unjust, I express my righteous indignation by writingLetters to the editor of The Pilot, ourLocal newspaper.

I'dLike to seeLess intransigent partisanship. This causes radicalism and unreasonable and extreme positions where cooperation becomes virtually impossible and progress is stymied. In the United States today, we have too much extremism.

There is such a thing as "the rule ofLaw." A democratic country is governed byLaw and not people. The future of our country is based upon the rule ofLaw and not the rule of individuals. Just because you don't approve of aLaw doesn't mean you can disobey it.

I'dLike to see more civility in our world today, starting in Washington, DC and replacing all the harsh rhetoric now being spewed. I'd alsoLike to see move civility in state andLocal politics and within corporations where corporate greed has permeated its ranks. Finally, there needs to be civility among family and friends. People in our country seem to haveLost good manners. Empathy can be a major ingredient for creating civility.

Chapter Six
Closing Thoughts and Items of Interest

Dief: What am I here for? Will myLife make a difference? These are difficult questions to answer. Would I be happy or fulfilled if I thought I had only existed and existed purely for my own gratification? Would I feel that myLife was a success if I were just an excellent golfer, a good story teller, a financial wizard, an avid reader, a wonderful dancer or well-known gourmet? If I reached these personal achievements from which I derived a great deal of personal satisfaction would I truly say myLife was worthwhile?

For me, this is not my view ofLeading a worthwhileLife. Rather I see myLife as being aLoyal and devoted husband to a woman ILove dearly. How fortunate am I to have had herLove and companionship for 55 years. She is the mother to our two children and has been a model mother for which I am most thankful. She has been a blessing in all ways.

Hopefully, I have been a good father to our children and grandfather to our grandchildren. They are certainly the apple of my eye and I am extremely proud of them. If there is any good in me, I would hope that it would rub off on them and theirLives will be better because of me.

I do know that because of my business career that the people in our office made it possible for more families to stay together because of theLife insurance that was payable at the death of the breadwinner. We also made it possible for hundreds, if not thousands, of people to retire with dignity because of the retirement planning we provided to them.

On a personal note, I think Evelyn and I, through our philanthropic efforts, have had a positive influence on many children and also on the educational proficiency of many teachers. I think ourLives have made a difference and we will be remembered for many years for our thoughtfulness and generosity. Is the world aLittle better because weLived? I would hope so. We tried!

Evelyn: Contentment is the word I would use to describe myself. I can't complain about anything in myLife. It has been almost too good to be true. Sometimes it's scary that everything has gone so well—a wonderful family and very good friends—something bad has to happen sometime, but so far it hasn't happened to me. I have really been blessed by God's grace and I'm certainly very thankful for that.

My father always said, "Where there isLove and faith there will be happiness." My mother used to say, "Be good and you'll be happy." They believed that if you work hard you will succeed. I also believe that, "If at first you don't succeed, try, try again."

Success can be thought of as how many true friends you really have and how many different people you are capable ofLoving. For financial success, you need a good attitude, good habits, and the knowledge you need to perfect your skills. For me, inner success means to be comfortable with who you are and what you stand for. Such inner success has given me peace of mind and contentment.

I pray that our children and grandchildren willLive by the values that have helped us in ourLives, especially the Golden Rule and the Ten Commandments.

What are your hopes for the next ten years?

Dief: For my wife and me to be able to watch our grandchildren establish their careers, get married and present us with great grandchildren. Also, I hope our health holds up reasonably well for the rest of ourLives so we don't become crippled and highly dependent on others to take care of us. That politicians becomeLess political and make decisions based on what's right and what's wrong; that many more countries become democracies; that moral values will be improved and we'll avoid becoming a decadent society.

Evelyn: I wouldLike for Dief and me to be reasonably healthy and that we will never be a burden to our children. That all of our wonderful grandchildren will have meaningful and happyLives, and that there will be peace on earth in theirLifetime. I wouldLike to see more kindness. I have a pillow that is cross-stitched with a saying that ILike:

So many Gods, so many creeds
So many paths that wind and wind
When just the art of being kind
Is all this sad world needs.

For a sixth grade social studies assignment in 1995, Dief's grandson, Steven McGinigle, researched and wrote a report about his grandfather "because Poppy is very fun

and interesting and is an important person in our family."
As part of the project, Steven sentLetters to seven people
to get additional information. Here are their responses
to questions about Dief's best characteristic and how he
makes people feel when they are around him.

DickLudlow (friend from childhood):

"By far, your Poppy's best characteristic was his ability to deal with people and maintain so many good friends. He makes me feel wonderful when I'm around him. He is not only my oldest and closest friend, but he is also my closest confidant in every part of myLife from the personal to financial and every other phase."

Peter Patrissi (employee):

"Your grandfather is a warm friendly person. EveryoneLikes him. He makes you feel good about yourself. He has a great and positive attitude and it rubs off on you. He is generally very easy going, but if you make him angry, watch out."

Bill Wallace (business colleague):

"Your grandfather is a truly wonderful person. He was a realLeader in our business and served as a role model for many. I admire him in many ways—

Monroe and Evelyn Diefendorf

> mostly for his character and hisLove of people. You won't go wrong paying attention to what your grandfather says."

Lee Broglio (brother-in-law and college roommate):

> "Poppy is generous, considerate and courteous. He is comforting to be around and he always respects you. That always makes you feel good."

Neil Gallagher (friend from college):

> "I didn't meet your grandfather until we were getting out of Amherst but we hit it off quickly and have been close friends for more than forty years. He cares, heListens, he is veryLoyal and he makes you feel comfortable. You are fortunate to have such great grandparents."

Judd Diefendorf (brother):

> "Your grandfather's best characteristic is that he takes an optimistic view of the world. HeLoves the good people that are around him and he sees the good points in people. When I'm around him he makes me feel upbeat and at ease. He gets frustrated at assembling something mechanical, but heLoves to tell about it. Your Grandma solves the problems—a good reason for getting married."

Bob Zucker (cousin):

> "Poppy has a good sense of humor. He is very easy to get to know and very comfortable to be with. He is a great idea man. In fact, he is good at getting great ideas and then talking someone else (like me) into doing them. This way if it goes wrong he doesn't get into trouble. There is aLesson in here for you!"

(Article reprinted from the MONY News, 1984)

GAMC Inducts Mgr. Diefendorf into Management Hall of Fame

New York General Manager Monroe M. Diefendorf, CLU was inducted into the Agency Management Hall of Fame of the General Agents and Managers Conference (GAMC) during a special ceremony held at the Fairmont Hotel in San Francisco, Calif. Mr. Diefendorf is the second MONY Manager to be given this honor.

Mr. Diefendorf was selected by his peers in theLife insurance industry for this prestigious honor, given to only one individual each year, in recognition of excellence in his profession and outstanding service to his industry and his community.

The Hall of Fame induction ceremony is a major event of the three-dayLife Agency Management Program (LAMP) meeting sponsored by the GAMC. More than 1,000 insurance Agency Managers and representatives of allied industry organizations attended this event in honor of Mr. Diefendorf.

Mr. Diefendorf began his career in theLife insurance industry in 1948, when he joined MONY as a Field Underwriter. He was named Manager of his present Agency in 1961, and was named Permanent General Manager in 1978. Under his direction, the Agency has consistently ranked in the top 10 of MONY's 175 Agencies nationwide. To date, Mr. Diefendorf hasLed the New York Agency to Topper status for 23 consecutive years. In 1983, his Agency produced approximately $100 million in commissions, and was the number one Agency in equity sales production.

He served on the Board of Directors of the GAMC from 1970 to 1974, and served as President from 1974 through 1975. He is also a former Director and President of theLife Managers Association of New York, which presented Mr. Diefendorf with its Ralph G. Engelsman award in 1975 for his dedication and devotion to theLife insurance industry. In 1979, he was elected a Trustee of the American College. Currently he serves as Chairman of the Research Agencies Group.

Instrumental in the development of the Agency Management Training Course (AMTCO), Mr. Diefendorf has served as Chairman of the Course in New York City. He has also served as a member of the American College's Chartered Financial Consultant Curriculum Committee, and as Chairman of the Designation Committee. He is a Charter,Life and Qualifying member of the National Management Award, having attained that Award every year since its inception in 1973.

Mr Diefendorf has spoken at numerous insurance conferences including the annualLAMP meeting, regional agency management conferences, andLocal GAMC,Life Underwriter Association and CharteredLife Underwriter meetings nationwide. He has been a frequent contributor to insurance trade journals, winning the award for "Best Article" twice.

A graduate of Amherst College, Amerherst, Mass., Mr. Diefendorf holds a B.A. degree. He interrupted his college studies to serve for three years in the U.S. Navy, asLieutenant on the Aircraft Carrier USS Nassau. He earned his CharteredLife Underwriter designation in 1962.

The GAMC Agency Management Hall of Fame was established in 1974 to recognize those individuals who have served as outstanding examples to their peers as topLeaders in agency building, insurance industry services and community support. Mr. Diefendorf's achievements mirror the standards by which all Hall of Fame members are measured.

(An editorial reprinted from the Brooklyn Daily Eagle
November 7, 1931)

The Eulogy of Warren T. Diefendorf

For two generations an outstanding citizen of Brooklyn, Warren T. Diefendorf passes at the age of 71. A native of Sharon springs, educated in up-State schools, a dry goods clerk at Fort Plain, organizer of a garment manufacturing company at the age of 23, he was in theLife insurance business before he was 27. For more than 40 years, he was in charge of the Brooklyn Agency of the MutualLife, and his success was regarded as phenomenal.

Mr. Diefendorf was a member of several clubs, active in the Knights of Pythias, energetic in pushing the work of the Brooklyn Chamber of commerce, a faithful MethodistLayman, a Thirty-second Degree Mason.

Never dogmatic never aggressive, wise in counsel, Warren T. Diefendorf will be missed by the organizers of good citizenship and progress in Brooklyn and onLong Island. He deserved well of this community.

Warren T. Diefendorf died on November 6, 1931. The funeral service was held on the evening of Monday, November 9th, at the Chester Hill M. E. Church, Mount Vernon, NY. Dr. Wallace H. Finch, Pastor of the church, delivered the eulogy which is reprinted on the following pages.

There are times in theLife of every minister of religion, when called upon to express some thoughts of comfort in the presence of death, or to voice some tribute of appreciation of aLife that has passed, that he finds himself in the grip of a great embarrassment. The only solace that can be offered are those general consolations of religion, and the only tribute that can be truthfully spoken is a tribute to qualities that are possessed by all.

But tonight our embarrassment arises from an entirely different source. Mr. Warren T. Diefendorf was a man who cannot be understood at all, apart from those powerful convictions of a deeply religiousLife. He possessed, indeed, his full share of those qualities which, in the field of moral adventure, a man develops only through commerce with the unseen ar.d the eternal.

Let is be said simply, and once for all, that he was a Christian man. That was quite the deepest and most significant thing about him. He inherited traits and characteristics from his human ancestry, as we all do, that marked out the natural inclinations of his mind, channeled the current of his spirit and gave direction to the interests ofLife that were to claim him. But this natural endowment is not sufficient to explain the influence he achieve, the hold he won upon our affections, and the impression his character made upon us.

Few are so fortunately born that they can dispense with self-elected cultures and disciplines to bring theirLives into harmony with the best. He would have been the first to disclaim any such fortune and first to confess that what he cherished most had come to him, not by gift of nature, but through those exercises and fellowships in religion, which, asLife advanced, had become his second nature.

He came into the fellowship of this church aLittle more than 29 years ago. During all those 29 years, there has been no time that one interseeds in this particular organization, could think of it without including in his thought the value and meaning of his presence here, his interest in its success, the ideals he cherished for it, the undoubtedLoyalty and devotion he freely gave to it.

Others might grow weary and fall from active participation in its enterprise or, displeased with some feature of its administration, withdraw their presence and their support but, through it all, the struggles incident to the development of a comparatively new congregation, the changing human personnel, the fluctuations of favorable and adverse circumstances and conditions, he stood faithfully and hopefully for it. And now you cannot tell the story of theseLast 29 years of this Christian enterprise in this city of Mount Vernon apart from his notable devotion to it. In thisLies the clue to his character. His ChristianLife, already mature and consistent when he came to this city 29 years ago, blossomed and fruited here. In that sense one who was our own has gone from us.

I could wish that one more competent than I might dwell for a few moments upon the mysterious blending of qualities that in their sum total constituted his personality, though I am grateful for the opportunity to relate simply what I have seen and understood.

Whenever I think of him I call to mind a certain quality of Gallantry! That implies both courage and courtesy. Courage not rude or unrumored but courage that is schooled in gentleness and refined by instinctive good-breeding and discipline. Courage not theLess real because it is gentle. For years he had carried the knowledge that the illness from which he died had marked him for its own. That wound, though he knew it to be mortal, he carefully hid from the sight of men. Insofar as he could manage it, that knowledge was never permitted to cast its spell upon his social relationships or its shadow upon his domestic or religious associations. In the hours when he was free from pain, no spirit could be more buoyant or contagious in its friendliness. When physical pain and distress denied him that privilege, he was still urbane and self-possessed, the true and courteous gentleman. He knew that the summons might come to him very suddenly, and he knew that it would come soon, but that knowledge did not intimidate him.

For aLong time, and under theLimitations of physical endurance that would have confined many a man to his home, if not to his bed, he would go, with a flower in hisLapel and a kindly smile upon his face, to his place of business in Brooklyn, that those who trusted in, and needed, him might not be denied.

Eight years ago, the gentleLady who had given her heart and hand to his keeping forLife and whose inspiring companionship had made his home a haven for his children and a center of gracious hospitality for his friends, passed from his side. Physically absent, her presence did not depart and on many an occasion, in speaking of her to some friend ofLater days, an expression of wistful tenderness would come to his face and a note of gentleness to his voice that betokened the inviolable bonds in which they were united.

The gallantry his presence suggested was not an external habit, worn to impress the beholder. It was a quality of the soul. It was of the very substance ofLife, the warp and wolf of his nature. As I think of his sufferings at theLast and the spirit in which he met them, I think of the dramatic poet and his Cerano de Bergerac saying:

> "You have wrested from me everything,Laurel as well as rose. With your wills; spite of your worst, something will still beLeft me to take whither I go. And tonight when I near God's house, in saluting, broadly will I sweep the azure threshold, with what despite of all, I carry forth untarnished and unbent, and that is—My Plume!"

Any appraisal of the qualities of our friend which failed to mention his characteristic response to the human appeal would be fatal to its justice. Men trusted him because he trusted them. If one betrayed his trust, it wounded him far more deeply than the pecuniaryLoss involved could possibly explain. I recall one night, some time ago, when calling at his home I found him in great depression of spirit. At once I attributed it to his illness, then, after a time, he told me, "It is not that. One of my men has failed me," and then, with some show of impatience, brushing aside the suggestion of the pecuniaryLoss involved, he said, "It isn't that, I tell you, I trusted him, can't you understand? I trusted him and he failed me!" It was that failure at the point of human trust that hurt him more.

That response to the appeal of the humanLed him to sponsor and support various enterprises in reclaiming the flotsom and jetsom of the human sea. ItLed him to identify himself with groups and organizations which have as their object some clarification of the problem of human relationships or some demonstration of the spirit in which that progress is to be found. ItLed him to fill his home with books that shed someLight on the tangled skein of social and personal problems and suggested methods and techniques in which the dawn of a better day could be introduced. It was his keen interest in the human that made him an eager traveler, around the world and across the seas; and, wherever he was, it was the human element that enchained his attention and that furnished him material for subsequent reflection. HeLoved beauty as ardently as a girl. But his response to it was no swift emotional sensation that burned itself up in its passing. It was grounded in a wholesome matter-of-factness that demanded thatLife as well as art should be beautiful.

Back of his successful career in business, this part of him, I doubt not, played an important role. He seemed to recall his clients, not as clients, but as men and women; his associates, not as business associates, but as friends. The good name of his company was an asset that was not for sale. There was a kind of universality about him that freed him from pettiness. His primary interest in men was not, "Is this man a Jew or a Gentile, a Protestant or a Catholic, but is he a man?"

This is not at all to suggest that he was devoid of convictions. He cherished some ideals and convictions that were imbedded very deeply in his nature. He had his convictions and stood by them. But just as he claimed the right to stand firmly by his own, he granted that right to others and respected them most when they exercised it. This is true toleration. The man without convictions is never tolerant; he is simply spineless. This man was far too deeply interested in humanLife to be without convictions. His convictions gave edge to his character, depth to his urbanity, and grace to hisLiving.

It is inevitable that in the presence of his passing, the age-old question should suggest itself, "If a man dies, shall heLive again?"

No one can answer that question for another. And no answer can possibly change the fact. Sometimes we hear men saying, "O, I do not believe in a futureLife. When we die that is the end of us." And they say it with an inflection and with an air of finality that seems to suggest that they are settling that question once for all.

Of course, the obvious reply to statementLike that is that what you believe or what you wish may have nothing at all to do with it. We were not consulted as to our wish or our belief about coming here. And it is manifest that we are not to be consulted as to the future. But if our beliefs cannot alter the fact, obviously they have much to do with our characters. If a man believes that he is toLive forever, there are some kinds of a man he will not want to be. If he believes that the future shall be in some true sense a redressing of the balance between the evil and the good, there are some things he will not want to do, and others that he most earnestly will desire to do. This man believed in a futureLife. That belief was integral to his nature and his religion. Since friendship meant so much to him here, he confidentlyLooked for its continuance there. SinceLove for his own was so deep within him here, he expected its consummation there. Since he had found beauty and truth so much a part of the presentLife, he had confidence that they are inseparably a part of theLife that is to come.

"It is very beautiful over there," said the great inventor and humanist, Edison, rousing from a deep sleep that hadLasted for hours, just prior to his death. In some such fashion our friendLying here tonight, touched by the majestic solemnity of death into silence, said to me a few days before the end came, as I sought to rally him with the hope of getting better, "No!Let's not deceive ourselves. This is myLast illness." Then, after a moment of silence, he added with a characteristic smile, "There is no illness where I am going."

And so, our uppermost emotion tonight is not of grief, sorrow, sadness. We mourn theLoss of a gallant companion of the way. We sorrow when we recall how sharp was the suffering he endured. We are sad when we think of the place in the home, in the Church, in the community, and in the office that will be vacant. But above these is another emotion. It is that of Thanksgiving, of Praise to God for a triumphant and victoriousLife. Were there a trumpeter here, it would be fitting that he should stand forth and sound, not taps for the dead, but a brave blast upon a silver trumpet of Victory and Peace.

"For all the saints who from theirLabors rest,
Who, thee, by faith before the world confessed,
Thy name, O Jesus, be forever blessed!"

"Thou was their rock, their fortress, and their might;
Thou,Lord, their captain in the well-fought fight;
Thou, in the darkness drear, their one trueLight."

"O blest communion, fellowship divine!
We feebly struggle, they in glory shine;
Yet all are one in thee, for all are thine."

"And when the strife is fierce, the warfareLong,
Steals on the ear the distant triumph song,
And hearts are brave again, and arms are strong."

"The golden evening brightens in the west;
Soon, soon to faithful warriors comes thy rest
Sweet is the calm of Paradise the blest."

"ButLo, there breaks a yet more glorious day;
The saints triumphant rise in bright array;
The King of glory passes on his way."

"From earth's wide bounds, from ocean's farthest coast,
Through gates of pearl streams in the countless host,
Singing to Father, Son, and Holy Ghost,
'Hallelujah, Hallelujah!"

Timeline of Life Events

1891, March 13 Dief's mother born (Martha Catharine Diefendorf)

1893, May 27 Dief's father born (Warren E. Diefendorf)

1901, March 15 Evelyn's father born (Frank Broglio)

1904, June 26 Evelyn's mother born (Lillian Glauda Broglio)

1924, July 18 Monroe Mechling Diefendorf born

1928, Dec 25 Evelyn Broglio Diefendorf born

1935, June 16 Dief's father died (Warren E. Diefendorf)

1942, Sept OurLady of Mercy Academy

1944, Sept Friends Academy

1946, Sept Skidmore College

1941 Sept-June '42 Stony Brook School

1942 June-Apr '43 Amherst College

1943 Nov-Oct '44 Williams College, Navy V-12 Officers Training Program

1944 Nov-Mar '45 Midshipman's School, Notre Dame University

1945 Mar-June '45 AdvancedLine Officer's School, Hollywood Beach, Florida

1945 June-Aug '46 Gunnery Officer, USS Nassau CVE-16 Pacific Duty

1946 Sept-June '47 Amherst College

1947 June-Aug '47 Williams College Summer School

1949, April 16 Monroe and Evelyn married

1950, June 5 Martha Jane Diefendorf born

1951 Move into house in Brookville

1952, Feb 7 Monroe Mechling Diefendorf Jr. born

1968 Martha graduates from Jericho High School

1970 Roey graduates from Deerfield Academy

1972 Martha graduates from Mount Holyoke College

1974 Roey graduates from Bucknell University

1974 Roey and Chris married

1974, Sept 1 Dief's mother died (Martha Catharine Diefendorf)

1975 Martha receives masters degree from UNC

1976 Roey receives masters degree from Georgia State

1977 Bought condo in Pinehurst

1987, August 19 Evelyn's father died (Frank Broglio)

1988 Bought house in Pinehurst

1989 Sold Brookville house

1990, April 14 Martha and Bob married

1998, Nov. 2 Evelyn's mother died (Lillian Glauda Broglio)

The years have gone by quickly. Much has been accomplished in myLife with Evelyn and hopefully much more has yet to be accomplished. But what would ourLives have meant if they were so quickly forgotten without passing on theLessons we haveLearned? Our forefathers sacrificed greatly to make thisLand a better place for you and me. I hope that we have contributed in a similar fashion for our family, friends and colleagues.

So, as my time on earth draws to a close, I am glad that we had the opportunity to purposefully put together the tapestry of ourLives in this book for those who follow.

We pray that our beliefs and thoughts will help youLead more productiveLives and will bring you a rich and rewardingLife filled with unlimited happiness. Success and happiness in thisLife will only come to you as you give yourself away to others. Remember, it is not how much you areLoved, but how much you haveLoved others.

— *Monroe "Dief" Diefendorf*

About the Author

"The Foundation" was established by Roey Diefendorf in an effort to capture, preserve, protect, and perpetuate ones "Personal Wealth ". Each family's "story" is told by their family in their own way in the form of a "Personal Legacy Manuscript." To insure that this valuable document is created, The Foundation provides a "Manuscript Advocate" who will guide a family through the process from start to finish. We help you determine your goals for preserving your personal wealth. We help determine your books' format and concept. Our "Legacy Questionnaire" is the first step in the process. Follow up personal interviews help to fill in the details. The manuscript writing, editing and layout are all part of the process. The end result is a professionally produced book designed to pass on your values for the generations that follow.